CONTEMPORARY'S

Put English To Work

LEVEL 4

INTERACTION AND COMPETENCIES FOR JOB SUCCESS

W9-BYG-030

CAROLE ETCHELLS CROSS

SERIES ADVISOR
CAROLE ETCHELLS CROSS

CONTEMPORARY BOOKS

a division of NTC/CONTEMPORARY PUBLISHING GROUP
Lincolnwood, Illinois USA

Publisher: Steve VanThournout
Editorial Director: Cindy Krejcsi
Executive Editor: Mary Jane Maples
Editor: Michael O'Neill
Contributing Writers: Laura Franklin, Jeffrey P. Bright
Design Manager: Ophelia M. Chambliss
Cover and Interior Design: Michael Kelly
Fine Art Illustrations: Adam Young
Line Art Illustrations: David Will
Production Manager: Margo Goia

Acknowledgments begin on page vi, which is to be considered
an extension of this copyright page.

ISBN: 0-8092-3356-8

Published by Contemporary Books,
a division of NTC/Contemporary Publishing Group, Inc.,
4255 West Touhy Avenue,
Lincolnwood (Chicago), Illinois 60712-1975 U.S.A.
© 1996 Carole Etchells Cross

0 1 2 3 4 5 6 7 8 9 DBH 16 15 14 13 12 11 10 9 8 7 6 5 4 3

Contents

Identifying skills needed for specific types of jobs • Identifying potential jobs corresponding to one's skills • Writing letters of application • Acquiring and evaluating information • Functions: Making offers; talking about work experience • Verb + pronoun + infinitive • Present perfect

Understanding job market trends and areas of job growth • Preparedness for job interviews • Understanding and completing a job application form • Acquiring and evaluating information • Understanding social systems • Functions: Describing ongoing activities and completed actions; requesting information; talking about possibility • Present perfect simple and continuous • Embedded questions • *May* and *might*

Understanding the basic function of social security • Interpreting government documents on social security • Interpreting and completing a social security form • Understanding social systems • Functions: Describing; expressing sympathy; recommending • Adjectival clauses with *who* • Embedded questions and complex sentences with *how*, *if*, and *whether* • *Should*

Preparedness for job interviews • Reading basic job descriptions • Reading career-information documents • Responding to difficult or unusual interview questions • Working with cultural diversity • Functions: Expressing obligation; recommending • *Supposed to* • *Might* for recommendations

Understanding paychecks and deductions for taxes • Understanding the basic range of employee benefits, including paid holidays, insurance plans, and unpaid leave • Reading employee benefits manuals • Acquiring and evaluating information • Understanding social systems • Functions: Comparing and contrasting; reporting what someone has said • *As . . . as* • Reported speech

Understanding job descriptions and responsibilities • Understanding job procedures and work flow • Describing one's job duties orally and in writing • Allocating human resources • Allocating time • Understanding organizational systems • Functions: Describing; identifying • Adjectival clauses with *that* and *which* • Past perfect

Put English to Work is a seven-level interactive workplace-literacy course for students of English as a second or foreign language. The series spans the entire range of levels usually taught in ESL/EFL programs—from the beginning-literacy level to the high-advanced level. A communicative, competency-based program, *Put English to Work* features an integrated syllabus focusing on workplace competencies, general English-language skills, communicative functions, form, and culture. The content of each text has been carefully planned to meet the curricular, instructional, and level requirements of California's state standards for adult ESL programs.

The format of *Put English to Work* is designed for maximum flexibility and ease of use. Teachers in a variety of programs—from vocational ESL and workplace ESL programs to general ESL programs with a school-to-work focus—will find this series ideal for their instructional needs. In addition, teachers who work with multilevel classes will find these texts useful with almost any combination of levels because of the cross-level coverage of a number of the most important workplace topics. *Put English to Work* consists of the following components:

- Seven student books, from Literacy Level to Level 6
- Seven teacher's guides, one for each level
- Seven audiocassettes, one for each level

Each student book contains a Picture Dictionary at the back—an additional resource offering teachers a variety of strategies for vocabulary building. The teacher's guides contain extension activities, sample lesson plans, and suggestions on adaptation of the materials to a number of different teaching styles and programs, from integration of grammar to using the materials in multilevel settings. The teacher's guides also contain the tapescripts for the audiocassettes, which are available separately.

The philosophy behind *Put English to Work*—spelled out in greater detail in the teacher's guides—is interactive and competency-based. The series places a strong emphasis on developing the four language skills—listening, speaking, reading, and writing—in conjunction with critical thinking, problem solving, and computation skills. An important feature is the incorporation of the SCANS competencies, developed by the Secretary's Commission on Achieving Necessary Skills in a project sponsored by the Department of Labor. In addition, the series focuses on a great number of the competencies within the Comprehensive Adult Student Assessment System (CASAS).

Skills are taught within an integrated framework that emphasizes meaningful and purposeful use of language in realistic contexts to develop communicative competence. Target language, structures, and functions are presented in contexts that are relevant to students' lives. Students need to learn strategies and skills to function in real-life situations—in particular, those related to job search and the workplace. Other situations and life-skill areas are covered as well, notably health, family, and community resources.

The cultural focus of *Put English to Work* not only presents aspects of U.S. culture that many students need to come to grips with, but also allows for a free exchange of ideas about values and situations that people from different cultures naturally view differently. In the process, students learn about the culture that informs the U.S. workplace while understanding that their own cultural perspectives are intrinsically valuable.

Level 4 of *Put English to Work* is geared toward learners at the high-intermediate level. Students at this level can function satisfactorily in English in survival situations; they can participate in basic conversations, and they can already comprehend conversations with unfamiliar vocabulary. A certain number of the skills of Level 3 are reviewed in Level 4, and teachers with classes of mixed intermediate-level students may wish to use Level 4 in conjunction with the Level 3 text. With mixed beginning-level and intermediate-level classes, teachers may also wish to use the Level 2 text with this level. Suggestions for use of these levels are provided in the teacher's guides for these levels.

Level 4 focuses on the development of intermediate language skills, document literacy, critical thinking, and problem solving through the presentation of realistic workplace contexts, along with frequent use of collaborative-learning activities. These activities involve working in teams with a team leader, a team recorder, and a team reporter. Group work of this type translates into more effective cooperative learning. Students do paragraph writing at this level, though punctuation is not taught explicitly. Paragraph-writing activities involve a preparation stage with guided writing of individual sentences. In Level 4, glosses are provided for some, but not all, unfamiliar vocabulary.

The SCANS competencies targeted in Level 4 are the following:

Allocating human resources
Allocating material and facility resources
Allocating time
Allocating money
Acquiring and evaluating information
Interpreting and communicating information
Leadership
Working with cultural diversity
Understanding systems
Designing systems
Selecting technology, tools, and equipment
Applying technology to a task
Troubleshooting technology

Acknowledgments

The authors and publisher of *Put English to Work* would like to thank the consultants, reviewers, and fieldtesters who helped to make this series possible, including Gretchen Bitterlin, San Diego Community College, San Diego, CA; Ann De Cruz; Greta Grossman, New York Association for New Americans, New York, NY; Bet Messmer, Educational Options, Santa Clara, CA; Michael Roddy, Salinas Adult School, Salinas, CA; Federico Salas, North Harris Montgomery County Community College, Houston, TX; Terry Shearer, Houston Community College, Houston, TX. Special thanks to Mark Boone.

Unit 1
IDENTIFYING JOB SKILLS

Openers

Look at the illustration. How do the words below apply to what you see?

job search   job center   job seeker   files   ads

Ali is going through the help wanted ads in the newspaper. Have you ever looked for a job in the paper? What kind of information about a job can you get from a want ad? Are there some skills that are desirable in many different jobs?

1 Listen and Think

Listen. Then answer the questions with a partner.

1. What kind of job is Ali looking for?

2. What kind of work has Ali done before? In Jordan? In the U.S.?

3. How has Ali looked for a job?

4. Does Ali meet all of the requirements for the job he's looking for?

5. Where does Rita suggest Ali look for a job?

6. What do you think of Rita's idea? Have you ever tried it?

2 Talk to a Partner

Step 1. Practice the conversation with a partner.

A: I'm calling about a position in customer service.
B: Have you done any customer service work in the past?
A: Yes, I have. I've worked in a number of restaurants and
   I'm currently working at a hotel.
B: How long have you been in your current job?
A: I've been there about six months.
B: I see. Well, we're sending out applications to potential
   candidates. Would you like me to send you one?
A: Oh, would it be possible to arrange for an interview?
B: The personnel manager will look over the applications
   and then call you if she wants to set up an interview.
   Would you like me to send you an application?
A: Yes, please.

Step 2. With your partner, choose an ad from page 3 and have a conversation like the one above. Use your own work experience to answer the questions or make up some information.

3 Read and Think

Step 1. Read the text below.

Ali began going through the help wanted ads again. Instead of looking only for a certain job by title, he concentrated on the skills required for many different jobs. He noticed that some ads gave very detailed information about job duties, while others were more general in their description of duties and requirements. Some ads listed pay rates and working hours, and most ads indicated how much experience was required.

Step 2. With a partner, look at the ads on the next page. What are some of the specific work skills required for each job? What are some of the other requirements listed?

Sales
DRIVER/SALES

Los Angeles Ford authorized distributor. Req'd: Valid Commercial driver's lic with auto and sales/customer service exp call G. Ryan 758-9078

CUSTOMER SERVICE

Leggets, a growing S.F. based footwear and apparel co, seeks candidate for int'l customer service. Must be detail oriented, have xlnt commun skills. BA, international background prefd.

RECEPTIONIST
FRONT DESK

Heavy phones. Responsible. Detail oriented. Fast learner. Able to interact with customers. Bilingual Spanish/English helpful. Brooklyn. Fax resume to: Attn. Lydia 653-9828

TRUCK DRIVER

Drives light truck to deliver tablecloths and linens. Prepares all receipts/ collects payments. Loads & unloads trucks. Two years experience. Hours 6 a.m. to 4 p.m. $9.25/Hour. Overtime 1½. Interview in Rosemont. Send this ad and resume to: Job # 87309467, P.O. Box 989367, Rosemont, IL 60764

Vocabulary

BA (abbreviation) Bachelor of Arts degree (a four-year college degree)

detail oriented able to pay attention to and remember details; able to follow very specific instructions

xlnt commun skls (abbreviation) excellent communication skills

exp (abbreviation) experience

heavy phones the job requires answering many phone calls

people skills ability to get along well and communicate effectively with people

pref/prefd (abbreviation) preferred; not required but definitely helpful

proven track record successful work experience

req'd (abbreviation) required

Practice

Complete the sentences with the correct words and phrases.

excellent communication skills   required
detail oriented   proven track record   people skills

1. John didn't apply for the job when he found out that a college degree was

   _____*required*_____ because he didn't have one.

2. Alicia is very confident that she will get the salesclerk job. She has a

   _____ as a sales representative for another company.

3. Pedro has very good _____. The customers at the restaurant all like him
   very much.

4. I don't think Lin would be a good bookkeeper. She's not very _____.

5. A good secretary spends a lot of time speaking with clients and writing letters, so he or she must

   have _____.

4 Put It in Writing

Step 1. **Think about the skills that you have used and developed in your previous
and current jobs. List them under the categories below:**

Job Skills	Communication/People Skills	Special Training
Example:	fluent in French	nursing certificate

Step 2. **Now use the lists to write three sentences describing your job skills.**

Examples:
I can speak, read, and write French fluently.
I have a certificate in nursing from the Medical Training Institute in Vietnam.

1. _____

2. _____

3. _____

5 Listen and Speak

Step 1. Listen. Kim came across an interesting ad in the paper, but she doesn't meet all of the requirements.

A: This sounds like a great job for me. Clinical laboratory assistant—
full time—must have two years' experience including experience
supervising staff.

B: Do you have that kind of experience?

A: I have plenty of medical experience. I was a nurse in Taiwan,
but I've never worked in a lab.

B: Have you ever been a supervisor?

A: Sure. I supervised the nurse assistants that worked with us in the
hospital. I'd really like to get back into the medical field somehow.

Step 2. Practice the conversation with a partner.

Step 3. List the pros and cons (good points and bad points) of this job.

Pros	Cons

Step 4. Continue the conversation with your partner. Student B: Do you think this sounds like a great job for Kim? Do you think she should apply for it? Tell her what you think she should do. Student A: Do you agree with your partner? Tell him or her what you are going to do.

Step 5. Change roles and think of a job related to your own work experience and skills. Have a conversation similar to the one above.

6 Read and Write

Step 1. Choose one of the ads from this unit. Imagine that you are interested in applying for that job and that you meet all of the requirements listed in the ad.

Step 2. You need to send the employer a résumé with a cover letter. Write the first paragraph of your cover letter following the example. Remember to let the employer know that you meet all of the job requirements.

Example:

October 26, 1996

Dear Sir or Madam:

I read with great interest your advertisement for a Registered Dietitian in the *Los Angeles Times* of October 22. As you can see from my résumé, I am a registered dietitian, and I have extensive experience. I completed my Masters Degree at the University of Kentucky in 1992.

Step 3. Now find another ad for a job related to your work experience and skills. Write the first paragraph of a cover letter following the example above. Be sure to include the skills that qualify you for the position.

_____

_____

_____

_____

_____

_____

_____

Step 4. With a partner, compare your work.

Form and Function

1 Would you like me to send you an application?

Would you like	me him, her, it us, them	to send you an application?
My supervisor told	me, you him, her, it us, them	not to leave yet.

Examples

I **asked** her **to give** me a ride. She **told** me **to wait** outside.
Paco **warned** me **not to call** in sick today.

Practice 1

A. Listen. Each sentence has two verbs. Match the first verb you hear from the left-hand column to the second verb you hear from the right-hand column.

asked   to have
wants   to call
warned   to meet
invited   to be
told   to stay

B. Fill in the blanks with the correct forms of the verbs in parentheses.

1. Silvio (invite) _____*invited*_____ (Renata go) _____*Renata to go*_____ to the movies.

2. My husband (encourage) _____ (me apply) _____ for that job.

3. Nobody (expect) _____ (me get) _____ that job.

4. Her father (teach) _____ (her drive) _____ when she was sixteen.

5. Would you please (remind) _____ (them be) _____ here at 5:00 tomorrow?

6. Carla (warn) _____ (you not go) _____ on that road; it's dangerous.

7. We (want) _____ (him work) _____ on our team, but he's already on another team.

2 I have worked in a number of restaurants.

I, you, we, they	**have**	worked	there three years.
He, she, it	**has**	worked	there three years.
How long	**have**	I, you, we, they	worked there?
How long	**has**	he, she, it	worked there?
I, you, we, they	**have**n't	worked	there very long.
He, she, it	**has**n't	worked	there very long.

Examples

We **have waited** for you for over an hour already. How many times **has** Stan **applied** for that job? Martha and Stewart **haven't stayed** late once this week.

Practice 2

A. Listen. Circle the form of the verb you hear.

1. called   (have called)

2. played   have played

3. bought   has bought

4. had   has interviewed

5. have answered   haven't answered

6. seen   have seen

B. Fill in the blanks with the correct forms of the verbs in parentheses. Use any other words in parentheses correctly in combination with the verbs.

1. (look) I _____*have looked*_____ at this chart twice already, but I just don't understand it.

2. (meet) I know we _____ before, but I can't remember when.

3. (not) (see) Julio told me he _____ his family in Nicaragua for over five years.

4. (lose) (anyone) _____ a wallet? I found one in the locker room.

5. (apply) (not) (have) I _____ for six different jobs, but I _____ one interview yet.

6. (be) (Karl and Paulo) _____ late at all this week?

7. (got) Chen _____ two promotions since he started working in this department.

C. Work with a partner. Student A: Look at this page. Student B: Look at page 10. The chart below shows what several people have done over the last month to look for jobs. Some of the information is missing. Ask questions and complete the chart. Use the correct forms of the verbs.

Examples:

B: How many applications has Anna filled out?

A: She's filled out six applications.

B: Where has Bill had interviews?

A: At schools.

Person	Action	Number	Place
Bill	fill out applications have interviews make phone calls	4 _____ 6	_____ school _____
Anna	fill out applications have interviews make phone calls	6 _____ _____	_____ _____ _____
Felix	fill out applications have interviews make phone calls	_____ 3 _____	hospitals, clinics _____ doctor's offices
Sylvia	fill out applications have interviews make phone calls	8 2 _____	grocery stores, airlines, offices _____ airlines, offices, travel agencies

Work with a partner. Student B: Look at this page. Student A: Look at page 9. The chart below shows what several people have done over the last month to look for jobs. Some of the information is missing. Ask questions and complete the chart. Use the correct forms of the verbs.

Examples:

A: Where has Anna applied for jobs?

B: She's applied at factories and hotels.

A: How many applications has Bill filled out?

B: He's filled out four applications.

Person	Action	Number	Place
Bill	fill out applications have interviews make phone calls	____ 1 ____	restaurants, schools office buildings restaurants
Anna	fill out applications have interviews make phone calls	6 ____ 0	factories hotels ____
Felix	fill out applications have interviews make phone calls	14 ____ 22	____ hospitals, clinics ____
Sylvia	fill out applications have interviews make phone calls	____ ____ 30	grocery stores, airlines, offices ____ ____

D. On a separate sheet of paper, write two sentences about each of the people in the chart.

E. Role-play.

Student A: Imagine you are one of the people from the chart. Tell your partner what you have done this month to look for a job. Tell him/her whether you are satisfied with the results you have gotten so far. Is there anything else you are planning to do?

Student B: Try to help your partner by offering encouragement and making suggestions for other things he/she might try.

Add your own ideas and change roles.

Putting It to Work

1 Pair Work

Step 1. Listen to the people describing their job skills and choose the job from the list below that best matches their skills. Make notes of the skills for each job.

accountant	day care attendant	sales representative
lab technician	secretary	maintenance worker

Step 2. Go over your lists of skills with a partner. Do you agree? Are there any other skills that you think would be important for any of these jobs that the speakers didn't mention? Add them to your lists.

2 Pair Work

Step 1. Think about all the different jobs you have had since you started working. Make a list of those jobs by job titles.

Step 2. Exchange lists with a partner. Ask your partner about his/her work history. For each job, ask about:

- job skills
- responsibilities
- type of business
- working conditions
- working hours
- salary

Step 3. Make a note of any skills you discussed for more than one job. Have you ever done work similar to your partner?

Step 4. Pair up with another pair of classmates. Choose one of your partner's jobs on the list and take turns telling the other pair about it. Ask any questions you might have about the jobs that are discussed.

3 Group/Class Work

Step 1. Post all of the job titles and skills from your work on the previous page around the classroom. If there are any duplicate job titles, consolidate the skills from the duplicates under one job title.

Step 2. Circulate around the room and read about all of the jobs your classmates have had and discussed. Ask any questions you might have about any of the jobs or job skills you see on the lists.

Step 3. Form a Job Club. Another technique for job hunting is to meet with other people in your field and discuss strategies and ideas that have worked. In your class, find other people with work histories similar to your own and form groups of at least three and no more than six. Note: you may have to form a "Miscellaneous" group if there are people with experience that is very different from everyone else's.

Step 4. In your Job Club take turns discussing strategies you have used to look for work in your field. You can also discuss strategies you have heard about even if you have never tried them yourself.

Step 5. Each Job Club should tell the rest of the class which strategies their club thinks are the most practical for job hunting in their field. Are there any similarities among groups?

4 Culture Work

How do the job titles and skills you have discussed in class compare with similar job titles in your native country? Are similar skills required for the same jobs or are there different expectations? What about education and special training requirements for jobs in your country compared with similar jobs in the United States?

In general, which job skills do you think are considered the most important for working in the United States? Why do you think they are considered to be important? Do you agree that they are important?

Now compare those skills to your native country: which job skills do you think are considered the most important for working there? Why do you think they are considered to be important? Do you agree that they are important? How are these skills different from those in the United States? How are they similar?

As you discuss the above questions with the class, can you find similarities among any of the other countries or cultures with regard to skills that are considered to be important?

Before you came to the United States, did you have any stereotypes about U.S. workers? If so, what they were like? If so, have you changed your mind at all now that you have lived here for a while? Discuss these with the class.

Openers

Look at the picture. How do the words below apply to this picture?

salary   overtime   benefits

Where is Antonio? What do you think he's doing? Have you ever done this?

1 Listen and Think

Listen to the conversation and circle Yes or No.

1. Has Antonio been going directly to some companies to apply for a job?   Yes   (No)

2. Has Antonio been reading want ads to find a job?   Yes   No

3. Has Antonio been reading the *Occupational Outlook Handbook*?   Yes   No

4. Has Antonio taken any civil service tests yet?   Yes   No

5. Has Antonio found a job yet?   Yes   No

2 Talk to a Partner

Step 1. **Practice the conversation with a partner.**

> A: Hey, Bruno. You know what one of the
>   fastest-growing occupations is?
> B: No. What?
> A: Paralegals.
> B: How do you know that?
> A: I've been doing some reading at the library.
> B: Hey. Maybe you can become a librarian!
> A: It's possible, but it's not on my list of the
>   fastest-growing occupations!

Step 2. **Now substitute other occupations from the list of the top ten fastest-growing occupations below.**

Fastest-Growing Occupations

1. paralegals
2. medical assistants
3. home health aides
4. radiology technicians
5. data processing equipment repairers

6. medical records technicians
7. medical secretaries
8. physical therapists
9. surgical technologists
10. operation research analysts

---

3 Read and Think

Step 1. **Read the following want ad from the classified section of a daily newspaper:**

> **WANTED: DRIVERS**
> 1 year experience required. High school graduates. Home most weekends. Up to $20/hour. Apply in person between 9–4 p.m. Sanborn Trucking, 2666 Main St. No Phone Calls.

Step 2. **With a partner, look at the list of people below. One of these people is qualified to apply for the above job. Who is it?**

- a man who has finished college
- a woman who can work only on weekends
- a high school graduate who has never worked as a driver
- a high school graduate with two years of driving experience
- a man who has a part-time job three days a week
- a man who finished high school this year

Step 3. Read the headline of the newspaper article below. With a partner, try to predict the content of the article.

Job Outlook Good in Service Sector, Health Care, Computers

Step 4. Now read the newspaper article that goes with the headline.

Would you like to know what the trends will be in the U.S. job market? Current trends will probably continue for the next ten to fifteen years. Here are data from a number of recent surveys:

The computer industry is the fastest-growing employment area. People in high demand include software designers, systems analysts, and programmers.

Health care is also a top area of job growth. Among the people in high demand are registered nurses, orderlies, attendants, medical assistants, radiology technicians, medical records technicians, and home health-care workers.

Retail sales is a major growth area, with high demand for cashiers and salespeople. Experts expect that cashiers will be in especially high demand for the next ten years.

However, occupations are growing at different rates in different places. For example, the demand for machinists is growing in the South, but it is declining in the Northeast. The demand for nursing aides, orderlies, attendants, and other health-care workers is growing especially strongly in Florida, Illinois, New York, and California.

In any case, over ninety percent of future jobs will require education beyond a high school diploma. Vocational programs are in big demand because many of the strongest growth areas are in occupations that require vocational training.

Vocabulary

medical records technicians people who keep and maintain medical records
nursing aides people who assist or help nurses
orderlies hospital workers who do routine jobs
radiology technicians people who work with x-ray machines and other radiology equipment

software designers people who create software programs
systems analysts people who look at a company's system to develop a computer program for the company

Step 5. Look up the words below in the dictionary, and then reread the article.

current   trends   data   survey

Step 6. With a partner, look over the article again. Why does the writer use the words *However* and *In any case* (at the beginning of the fifth and sixth paragraphs)? Can you find any specific divisions in this text? What are they?

Complete the following sentences with the words below.

data   systems analyst   current   nursing aides   survey

1. If _____*current*_____ trends continue, the computer industry will continue to expand.

2. In order to figure out which jobs will be important in the future, a number of experts have done

    a _____ of businesses and organizations.

3. There will most likely be an increasing need for _____ in hospitals because there won't be enough nurses to do all the work.

4. LabComm Inc. decided to improve its record-keeping system, so the company hired a

    _____ to look at the company's organization and make some recommendations.

5. A study of 100 companies produced a lot of _____ that will provide an understanding of the business outlook for the future.

4 Put It in Writing

Step 1.   Choose one of the ads from Unit 1. Prepare to write a job letter to answer an ad. Write the date in upper left-hand corner, as shown below.

September 10, 1997 _____ *Date*

Wendy Haverson _____ *Name*
114 Green St. _____ *Street number and street name*
Chicago, IL 60645 _____ *City, state, and zip code*

Dear Sir or Madam: _____ *Greeting*

Step 2.   On a separate sheet of paper, write a short paragraph that tells which job you would like. Write a sentence that says where you saw the ad (use the name of your local newspaper, for example). Include the sentence "Enclosed please find my résumé."

Step 3. Add a sentence that gives your telephone number and a closing—a polite sentence that ends the letter. Then add your name at the end.

Example:

For more information, or to set up an interview, please call me at 678-5044.

Thank you for your consideration.

Sincerely,

Antonio Ferrer

Step 4. With a partner, exchange your work. Look at your partner's letter and correct any mistakes you find. Then discuss your partner's corrections.

5 Listen and Speak

Step 1. Listen to the job interview between Antonio and Mr. Russell of Russell Telemarketing.

Mr. Russell: Thanks for coming in, Antonio. Tell me something about yourself. Where have you been working this past year?

Antonio: At Langston Insurance in the city. My job is to telephone and locate insurance customers for the salesmen.

Mr. Russell: Interesting. And why do you want to leave the company?

Antonio: Frankly, I'd like to find a job with some advancement possibilities and maybe where I can earn some more money. I'm not going anywhere on this job I have now.

Mr. Russell: It would be possible for you to advance on this job, but only if you are willing to work hard.

Antonio: I'm a very hard worker, Mr. Russell.

Mr. Russell: I believe you are. And you're hired! Besides the excellent salary, you will find that we have good benefits and that there is some opportunity for overtime work in addition to a yearly bonus.

Antonio: Thanks, Mr. Russell. You won't be sorry you hired me.

Step 2. With a partner, practice the conversation.

Step 3. With your partner, role-play an interview between Bruno and Mr. Smyth for the position of auto detail person. Mr. Smyth may ask the following questions, but add your own questions also.

- What is your work experience?
- Why do you want to leave your current job?
- Why would you like to work for this company?
- Why do you think you would be a good employee?
- What are your strengths and weaknesses?

6 Read and Write

Step 1. Read the information about Antonio Ferrer.

Antonio Blas Ferrer was born in the Dominican Republic but has lived in New York City (zip 10025) at 306 West 103rd Street for several years. He has been working at Wallace Manufacturing Co. at 103 E. 42nd as a packer since 1992. He boxes the items coming off the production line. His supervisor is Fred Matson. Antonio is looking for a new job because he would like a position with some possibilities for promotion.

Step 2. Antonio Ferrer is applying to Universal Glass Company for a job. Fill out the following job application for him, using the information above.

UNIVERSAL GLASS COMPANY
APPLICATION FORM

Name _____*Ferrer*_____*Antonio*_____*Blas*____
                 Last   First   Middle

Address _____
                       City   State   Zip Code

Place of birth _____

U.S. Citizen? _____

Employer's Name and Address

_____

_____

_____

Job Title and Duties

_____

_____

_____

Year Started _____ Supervisor's Name _____

Step 3. With a partner, compare your work.

Form and Function

1 A: Haven't you been working on that all week?
   B: Yes, I have, and I've finally finished it.

I, you, we, they	**have** **haven't**	**been working**	on it all week.
he, she, (it)	**has** **hasn't**		
Have **Has**	I, you, we, they he, she, (it)	**been working**	on it all week?
How long have **has**	I, you, we, they he, she, (it)	**been working**	on it?

I, you, we, they he, she, (it)	**have/haven't** **has/hasn't**	**finished** it.
Have I, you, we, they **Has** he, she, (it)		**finished** it?
What have I, you, we, they **has** he, she, (it)		**finished?**

Examples

I**'ve been looking** for jobs all month, and I**'ve sent** out ten letters so far this week.
Ranjit **has been talking** to personnel managers, employment counselors, and lots of other people, but he **hasn't found** a job yet. We**'ve been talking** for hours, and we **haven't finished** our work.

Practice 1

A. Listen and circle the correct words.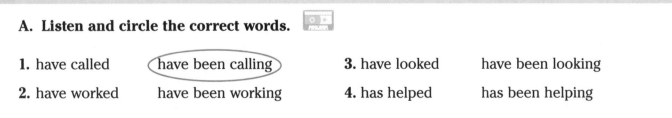

1. have called   (have been calling)   **3.** have looked   have been looking
2. have worked   have been working   **4.** has helped   has been helping

B. Choose the correct form of the verbs in parentheses. If more than one choice is possible, choose the *ing* form.

1. How many letters (you send) ___*have you sent*___ so far?

2. What (you do) _____ all day?

3. Gene and I (write) _____ to twenty companies already, and there are fifteen more on our list.

4. A: How long (you look) _____ for a job? B: About two months.

5. A: (You finish) _____ your résumé yet? B: No, I haven't.

6. A: (Sarah find) _____ a job? B: Yes, she found a job last week.

7. I (have) _____ interviews at ten companies so far, and I (talk)

   _____ to an employment counselor since August.

C. For each sentence with more than one possible answer, write a sentence with the other tense possible.

_____

_____

_____

_____

D. With a partner, compare the sentences you have written.

E. With a partner, talk about your efforts to find a job. Where have you looked? How long have you been looking? What kinds of jobs have you been looking for? If you have any recommendations for your partner, tell him/her.

2 Can you tell me what that company makes?

How long is lunch?	I'd like to know	**how long** lunch **is**.
When does break time **start**?	Can you tell me +	**when** break time **starts**?
How many did you **do**?	Tell me	**how many** you **did**.

Examples

Tell me **how you have been**.   (from "How have you been?")
I was wondering **what the pay is**.   (from "What is the pay?")
Can I ask **when benefits begin**?   (from "When do benefits begin?")
Please show me **where I sign**.   (from "Where do I sign?")

Practice 2

A. Listen to and read the pairs of questions. Do they mean the same thing,
or are they different? Mark = for *same* or ≠ for *different* for each one.

1. a. How much overtime did you work?   =   b. Do you know how much overtime you worked?

2. a. How often do the workers get paid here?   b. I'd like to know how often the workers get paid here.

3. a. What is my supervisor's name?   b. Can my supervisor say what my name is?

4. a. Where should I write my wife's name?   b. Show me where I should write my wife's name.

B. Change the word order from a regular question into an embedded question.
Then copy the new, long question onto a separate sheet of paper.

Example: How much **is the uniform fee**?

Who can tell me   how much ____the uniform fee is____?

1. Where **are the time cards**?   She doesn't know where _____.

2. Who **will my supervisor be**?   Could you tell me who _____?

3. What does **"liable" mean**?   Please explain again what _____.

C. With a partner, practice saying, embedded questions. Use introductory phrases and the question-idea phrases below. Do not change the word order of the question phrases. Say as many as you can in five minutes. Then write at least ten of these in your notebook.

Can you tell me	You should know
I'd like to ask	Nobody knows
Do you understand	I need to know
I'll tell you	My question is

3 There may be some job openings at that company. It probably has good benefits, and they may need someone.

There	**may be**	some job openings	(possible, maybe probable)
There	**might be**	some job openings	(possible, not probable)

Examples

A: That company **may be** a good place to work. B: It **might be**, but I doubt it.
A: Business probably will get better next year. There's a lot of consumer demand.
B: Well, business **may get** better, but we'll have to wait and see.
C: Business **might get** better, but it's more likely that it will get worse.

Practice 3

A. Listen. Circle the words you hear.

1. may (might)   **3.** may might   **5.** may might
2. may might   **4.** may might   **6.** may might

B. On a separate sheet of paper, write five sentences about job possibilities. Rank the jobs in order of probability and use *may* and *might*. You can also use *probably* or *possibly* with *will*.

C. Tell a partner about your job possibilities.

Example: I had a job interview last week at a plastics company. That's a job I may get. I had another interview two weeks ago. I might be able to get that job, too, but it's less likely.

Putting It to Work

1 Pair Work

Step 1. Interview a partner. Discuss your partner's job skills and tell him/her about yours. List your skills on a separate sheet of paper.

Step 2. With your partner, look at the chart below. How do your specific job skills fit the categories of the different industries on the chart? List your skills in the chart and match them to the categories. If you think there is a category missing, add it.

Manufacturing

1. Manual skills

2. Ability to operate machinery

3. Lifting and loading

Clerical Work

1. Typing skills

2. Filing and organizational skills

3. Basic knowledge of computers and other equipment

Restaurant Work

1. Customer service skills

2. Ability to work under pressure

3. Ability to work well with people

Health Care

1. Manual skills

2. Basic knowledge of medicine

3. Ability to work well with people

4. Organizational skills

Computers/Data Processing

1. Knowledge of computers and software

2. Strong problem-solving skills

Other

1.

2.

3.

4.

Step 3. With your partner, discuss the information in your charts. Is there anything you can add?

Step 4. With your partner, analyze the chart to see if your skills fall under several categories. If so, what other kinds of possibilities are there for you?

2 Group/Class Work

Step 1. Work with a group. Choose a team leader, a team recorder, and a team reporter. Use your information from the previous activity. Share your information with the whole group.

Step 2. Brainstorm a number of potential job areas for each member of the group. Record your information in a chart like the one below. List specific jobs and types of companies.

Student 1	Student 2	Student 3	Student 4

Step 3. Now rank the ideas you have discussed in order of greatest probability for each student. Discuss this ranking with the members of your group until you are in agreement.

Step 4. Your team recorder will tell the class your ideas. Listen to the ideas of the other teams and evaluate them. Tell the class what you agree with and what you disagree with.

3 Culture Work

With the class, discuss these questions:

What does it mean when someone has difficulty finding a job?
How much is an individual responsible for his or her success in finding a job?
How much help should an individual receive from society?
What aspects of the U.S. job market are the most difficult for new immigrants?
How can people best adapt to the job situation in the United States?
What advice would you give newcomers from your country?

Unit 3
SOCIAL SECURITY

Openers

Look at the pictures. Do the words below apply to the situations you see? How?

disability   co-workers   retirement

These are two changes in life that may happen to workers. Do you know anyone who has
been in these situations? Did you know that Social Security may be able to help people in
times like these?

1 Listen and Think

Listen and answer the questions below.

1. Tuyet is retiring.   Ⓣ   F

2. Tuyet is happy about the change in her life.   T   F

3. Jorge is retired.   T   F

4. Jorge is disabled.   T   F

5. Jorge receives Social Security.   T   F

2 Talk to a Partner

Step 1. Two employees are discussing Social Security. Practice the conversation with a partner.

A: How old is your father?

B: Oh, my father passed away several years ago.

A: Oh, I'm sorry to hear that.

B: Yeah, it was really tough at first.

A: I know how you feel. I lost my sister a year ago.

B: Oh, that's terrible! I'm sorry.

A: Well, I know how it is to lose a close relative. It's really hard to accept.

B: Yeah. And it was hard for us financially, too. My mother wasn't working when my father died.

A: Do you get Social Security?

B: Yes. We get our Social Security checks, but it's still difficult.

A: I know how you feel. But at least it's there. But when I see the F.I.C.A. deductions on my paycheck for Social Security, I have to wonder about it. I don't know if it will be there thirty years from now.

B: It probably will. The system is changing.

Step 2. Now, with the same partner, talk about the other situations when people receive Social Security. Do you know what those situations are? Role-play a similar conversation about Social Security in one of those situations.

3 Read and Think

Step 1. Read the text below and the box at the right.

Who receives money monthly from Social Security?

Each month, over 42 million people in America receive Social Security checks. They earned these benefit payments only because they (or their working family members) contributed to Social Security when they worked.

Who contributes money to Social Security?

Over 138 million workers in America are now contributing to the Social Security insurance system. They are putting their money into the system through payroll taxes that are taken from their paychecks like income taxes. Employers also contribute to the system in amounts equal to what employees pay.

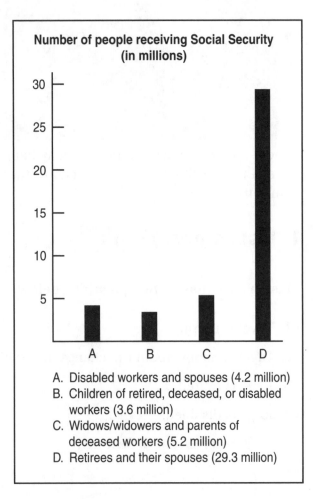

Number of people receiving Social Security (in millions)

A. Disabled workers and spouses (4.2 million)
B. Children of retired, deceased, or disabled workers (3.6 million)
C. Widows/widowers and parents of deceased workers (5.2 million)
D. Retirees and their spouses (29.3 million)

Step 2. With a partner, use the information on page 26 to answer the questions below.

1. How many people receive Social Security every month?

2. If a worker has never contributed to Social Security, will she receive benefit checks if she is disabled or when she retires?

Vocabulary

contribute (to) give, especially money, but not getting something back right away

deceased dead, no longer alive or living

deduction an amount taken out of one's pay or earnings

disability a condition that makes it impossible for one to work

disabled when one has a disability

F.I.C.A. Federal ("national") Insurance Contributions Act, the U.S. law that requires Social Security payroll deductions

mandatory required, usually by law or rule

payroll the system of paying workers and keeping track of who is paid how much for their work

retiree a person who stopped working (or **retired**) when he or she became old

self-employed working for oneself, with no employer making F.I.C.A contributions

spouse one's wife or husband

survivors the people who are still alive after others (relatives, townspeople) die

widow/widower a wife/husband whose spouse has died

Step 3. Read the boxes below.

A. The Development of Social Security	
1800s	Germany develops government-sponsored old-age and sickness insurance programs
1935	U.S. President Franklin D. Roosevelt signs into law the Social Security Act
1940	The first Social Security retirement payment of $22.54 goes to Ms. Ida Fuller of Vermont
1968 to 1977	Social Security benefit payments increase by 130 percent
1989	Average retirement benefits equal $537 per month
1994	Average retirement benefits equal $829 per month

B. Social Security Tax Rates	
Employee's contributions	The employer takes 7.65% of the worker's earnings (up to $61,200) as mandatory pay deduction to give to government.
Employer's contributions	The employer also pays 7.65% of the amount of the worker's earnings to the government for Social Security.
Self-employed person's contributions	People who are self-employed pay 15.3% of their earnings to the U.S. government when they pay income tax.

C. Full Retirement Benefits Age

This year: 65 years old
In 2022: 67 years old
In _____: 70 years old

Practice

Read each statement and circle T (True) or F (False).

1. The United States was the first country in the world to have government-sponsored social insurance. T (F)

2. The amount of Social Security benefit checks has increased over the years as life has become more expensive. T F

3. People who work for themselves must pay more money into Social Security. T F

4. A worker who retires in 30 years at the age of 65 will receive the highest possible Social Security benefit payments. T F

4 Put It in Writing

Step 1. Social Security numbers are important in the United States. Think about how you and others use your Social Security number. Tell the class about when and where you use your Social Security number. The teacher will write a list on the board.

Examples: When I get hired for a job
At a clinic (for identification)

Step 2. Copy the list from the board into your notebook.

Step 3. Now write three sentences about the uses of your Social Security number.

Example: When I first got my driver's license, I had to show my Social Security card.

1. _____

2. _____

3. _____

5 Listen and Speak

Step 1. Alex is explaining Social Security to Teresa. Listen to the conversation.

Alex: Look at this part of my check, where it says F-I-C-A. That's for Social Security.

Teresa: That's for retirement, right?

Alex: Yes, and disability. If you have an accident, for example, and you can't work anymore, you get Social Security.

Teresa: So how much do they take out?

Alex: 7.65 percent. And the company puts in the same amount.

Teresa: Do I need some special papers for this? I don't think I have any.

Alex: I know. But you weren't a company employee before. Now you'll definitely need a Social Security number. You'll need to go to a Social Security office. There are several around Los Angeles.

Teresa: Which office would be the best?

Alex: Let's see. You should go to the downtown office. It's faster and closer. And the people are OK there. I'll give you the address if you need it.

Step 2. Practice the conversation with a partner.

Step 3. With a partner, create an ending to the conversation.

Step 4. With another pair of classmates, compare your endings. How are they the same? How are they different?

6 Read and Write

Step 1.   Below are some official statements from the U.S. Social Security Administration. First read the headings. Then read the statements.

---

1.   Your Earnings Record

The Social Security Administration keeps a lifetime record of the earnings reported under your name and Social Security number. You can check your earnings record by calling 1-800-772-1213 and asking for a Personal Earnings and Benefit Estimate Statement.

2.   About Social Security Benefits

Social Security benefits are based on your earnings over your working career.

3.   You and Your Social Security Taxes

You and your employer pay an equal share of Social Security (F.I.C.A.) taxes. (The only exceptions are people who are self-employed or working for certain government or other special organizations.)

4.   Social Security Misuse

Sometimes more than one person uses the same Social Security number, either on purpose or not. It is against the law to use someone else's Social Security number or to give false information when applying for a number.

5.   If You Think Our Records Are Wrong

If you find that too much or too little is reported to your number, notify Social Security. We will help you correct your record. You should report any errors right away because the law only allows us to correct a Social Security record within 3 years, 3 months, and 15 days after the year in which the error occurs.

Step 2.   Now answer the following questions. Refer to page 29 to remember Teresa's situation.

1. What form should Teresa get from Social Security? _____

_____

2. If Teresa worked but her employer did not take out F.I.C.A. taxes, who should she contact?

_____

3. For what years can Teresa have her records corrected? _____, _____, and _____ only.

Step 3.   Practice filling out the form on page 31. You can call 1-800-772-1213 to ask Social Security for a current, official form.

SOCIAL SECURITY ADMINISTRATION
Application for a Social Security Card

Form Approved
OMB No. 0960-0066

INSTRUCTIONS

- Please read "How To Complete This Form" on page 2.
- Print or type using black or blue ink. DO NOT USE PENCIL.
- After you complete this form, take or mail it along with the required documents to your nearest Social Security office.
- If you are completing this form for someone else, answer the questions as they apply to that person. Then, sign your name in question 16.

1 NAME
To Be Shown On Card

FIRST	FULL MIDDLE NAME	LAST

FULL NAME AT BIRTH IF OTHER THAN ABOVE

FIRST	FULL MIDDLE NAME	LAST

OTHER NAMES USED

2 MAILING ADDRESS
Do Not Abbreviate

STREET ADDRESS, APT. NO., PO BOX, RURAL ROUTE NO.

CITY	STATE	ZIP CODE

3 CITIZENSHIP
(Check One)

☐ U.S. Citizen ☐ Legal Alien Allowed To Work ☐ Legal Alien Not Allowed To Work ☐ Foreign Student Allowed Restricted Employment ☐ Conditionally Legalized Alien Allowed To Work ☐ Other (See Instructions On Page 2)

4 SEX

☐ Male ☐ Female

5 RACE/ETHNIC DESCRIPTION
(Check One Only—Voluntary)

☐ Asian, Asian-American Or Pacific Islander ☐ Hispanic ☐ Black (Not Hispanic) ☐ North American Indian Or Alaskan Native ☐ White (Not Hispanic)

6 DATE OF BIRTH
MONTH DAY YEAR

7 PLACE OF BIRTH
(Do Not Abbreviate)
CITY   STATE OR FOREIGN COUNTRY   FCI

Office Use Only

8 MOTHER'S MAIDEN NAME

FIRST	FULL MIDDLE NAME	LAST NAME AT HER BIRTH

9 FATHER'S NAME

FIRST	FULL MIDDLE NAME	LAST

10 Has the person in item 1 ever received a Social Security number before?

☐ Yes (If "yes", answer questions 11-13.)   ☐ No (If "no", go on to question 14.)   ☐ Don't Know (If "don't know", go on to question 14.)

11 Enter the Social Security number previously assigned to the person listed in item 1.

☐☐☐ – ☐☐ – ☐☐☐☐

12 Enter the name shown on the most recent Social Security card issued for the person listed in item 1.

FIRST	MIDDLE	LAST

13 Enter any different date of birth if used on an earlier application for a card.

MONTH   DAY   YEAR

14 TODAY'S DATE ▶ MONTH DAY YEAR   **15 DAYTIME PHONE NUMBER** ▶ ( ) AREA CODE

DELIBERATELY FURNISHING (OR CAUSING TO BE FURNISHED) FALSE INFORMATION ON THIS APPLICATION IS A CRIME PUNISHABLE BY FINE OR IMPRISONMENT, OR BOTH.

16 YOUR SIGNATURE

▶

17 YOUR RELATIONSHIP TO THE PERSON IN ITEM 1 IS:

☐ Self ☐ Natural Or Adoptive Parent ☐ Legal Guardian ☐ Other (Specify)

DO NOT WRITE BELOW THIS LINE (FOR SSA USE ONLY)				
NPN		DOC	NTI	CAN	ITV
PBC	EVI	EVA	EVC	PRA	NWR	DNR	UNIT
EVIDENCE SUBMITTED				SIGNATURE AND TITLE OF EMPLOYEE(S) REVIEWING EVIDENCE AND/OR CONDUCTING INTERVIEW

DATE

DCL   DATE

Form **SS-5** (9/89)

3

Form and Function

1 People who are retired receive Social Security every month.

> Some people are retired. Those people receive Social Security.
>
> | People | **who are** retired | receive | Social Security. |
> |--------|---------------------|---------|------------------|
> | A person | **who is** retired | receives | |

Examples

A civil servant is <u>a person</u> **who works** in a government office. <u>Anyone</u> **who needs** a Social Security card <u>has</u> to go to a government office or file the forms through the mail.
U.S. <u>citizens</u> **who have worked** all their lives <u>expect</u> Social Security.

Practice 1

A. Listen and circle the words you hear. 🔲

1. who is (who are) 3. who is who are 5. who is who are

2. who is who are 4. who is who are 6. who is who are

B. Combine the sentences below. Use *who* with the appropriate verb forms.

1. People (receive) *who receive/who are receiving* Social Security have already paid into the system.

2. A manager (give) _____ his employees support is a good manager.

3. A civil servant (deal) _____ with a lot of people can become irritable.

4. A Social Security card is necessary for anyone (want) _____ to work in the United States.

5. People (pay) _____ into the system hope it will continue.

C. With a partner, talk about and describe someone you know. Use phrases with *who*.

Example: I have a neighbor who is very interesting. He's a man who works at the post office.

2 I'm so sorry to hear about that. I know how you feel.

How *do* **you feel?**   (I know.)

I know   **how**   **you feel.**

Is President's Day   a company holiday? (I don't know.)

I don't know *if* **President's Day is**   a company holiday.

Examples

Who knows **if Monday is** a holiday?   Do you know **whether or not we get** a year-end bonus?
I'll tell you **if you can go** home or not.   I wonder **if everyone knows** about the new uniform policy.

Practice 2

A. Listen and circle the words you hear.

1. (this is)   is this   **3.** you do   do you   **5.** she has   has she

2. you are   are you   **4.** they are   are they   **6.** we do   do we

**B. Change the word order from a regular question into an embedded question.
Then copy the new, long question.**

Example:

Is this regular or decaf coffee? *Do you know if **this is** regular or decaf coffee?*

1. Should I change my withholding allowances? I need to know if _____*I should*_____ change my withholding allowances.

2. Does everyone have to have a uniform? My main question is whether or not _____ to have a uniform.

3. What is the problem? I know what _____.

4. Did the night crew finish the Farley job? I need to know if _____ that job.

C. Work with a partner. Role-play the situation below. Use expressions with *I know how* or *I know what* with the questions below. Express sympathy. Change roles.

Questions: How do you feel? What's the problem? What's wrong? What's the situation?
Situation: Someone you know is very ill. You feel very bad about it.

3 You should go to the downtown office. It's faster and closer than the other ones.

I, you, he, she, it, we, they		**should** **shouldn't**	go	to the downtown office.
Should	I, you, he, she, it, we, they	**go**		to the downtown office?
Where should	I, you, he, she, it, we, they	**go?**		

Examples

There are several good places for me to apply for my Social Security number. **Where should I go?**
I think **you should go** to the office in the suburbs. You hardly ever have to wait there.

Practice 3

A. Listen and circle the places, people, or things that each person recommends.

1. the foreign car — the American car
2. the warehouse job — the office job
3. Kamil Jabal — Pedro Martinez

4. the office in the suburbs — the office in the city
5. Ed Grazer — Judy Alstrom
6. Los Angeles — New York

B. On a separate sheet of paper, write recommendations for a partner for two or three of the following things:

- a place to get a driver's license or state identification card
- a car dealer where you can get a good deal on a car
- a branch of the government where you can apply for U.S. citizenship
- a library where you can find books in foreign languages
- a place where you can find information about companies in your area
- a good restaurant that serves food from your country
- a good school for your children

C. Now tell your partner your recommendations and discuss your partner's recommendations.

Putting It to Work

1 Pair Work

Step 1. With a partner, read about the people below.

1. Mohamed's widow uses Social Security survivors' benefits to help support her children. But her mother-in-law is also in the family. Can she get more dependent benefits?

2. Oscar's brother-in-law, Jorge, receives disability benefits from Social Security. Now Oscar would like to find out what his benefits might be if he needed them.

3. Because Ted's immigration status was changed last year, he now works legally. He wonders if he can get Social Security credit for any of the eight years he worked here before that.

Step 2. With your partner, write three sentences using the phrases below to give advice or make suggestions for the three people above.

    I think you should . . .   Well, you could . . .
    My advice to you is to . . .   The best thing would be to . . .

1. _____

2. _____

3. _____

Step 3. Now, select one of the three situations to role-play. Practice speaking without looking at the page, and then present the role-play to the class.

2 Group/Class Work

The United States, like Canada and other English-speaking countries, is home to many immigrants. The attitudes that people in America have toward immigrants vary greatly.

Step 1. **Make a list of things that people in America say about immigrants. Indicate whether these comments are favorable, neutral, or unfavorable.**

Step 2. **Conduct a mock "public forum" on immigrants. Divide the class into three groups— those who will speak favorably, neutrally, and unfavorably about immigrants. Use the items from the list you developed in Step 1. Take turns giving speeches, reactions, statements of fact, etc.**

Step 3. **After the groups have presented their ideas, discuss what they have said.**

3 Culture Work

With your class, discuss the following questions:

1. What is the responsibility of society for individuals?
2. Should society help families? If so, how?
3. Should the government take care of people when they are old? If so, how?
4. Should everyone receive Social Security? If so, why? If not, who shouldn't?

Unit 4
DISCUSSING JOB SKILLS IN AN INTERVIEW

Openers

Look at the scenes below. Find these things:

waiting area	applicants	receptionist	file
counter	sign-in sheet	interviewer	

Tran is interviewing for a job at St. Joseph's Hospital. The interviewer is the Director of Radiology. Have you had any interviews recently? How did you feel? What kinds of questions did you have to answer?

1 Listen and Think

Listen to the interview. Then answer the questions with a partner.

1. Which job is Tran interviewing for?
2. Is this his first interview for this job?
3. What kinds of skills does Tran mention?
4. Which skills do you think Sandra Kelly wants? Why?
5. How does Tran describe his technical skills?
6. What else does Tran tell Sandra Kelly about? Why?
7. How do you think the interview went?

2 Talk to a Partner

Step 1. Raul is in a job interview. Practice the conversation with a partner.

A: Hello, my name is Mr. Calloway, and I understand you're interested in the assistant manager position.

B: Yes, that's right. My name is Raul Rodriguez.

A: Well, Raul, what interests you about the position?

B: I've been working in retail for several years now, and I feel I'm ready for more responsibility.

A: Have you ever supervised people before?

B: Yes, I have. Before I came to the United States I was the director of a small company in Mexico.

A I see. What other experience do you have that would help you in this position?

B: I'm very experienced with computers, I've worked a great deal with budgets, and I've had full responsibility for stock inventory for the past 18 months at my present job.

A: Hmm. OK, now tell me, what are your strong points?

B: My strong points? I'm very organized, I work hard, and I'm very serious about what I do.

Step 2. With the same partner, take turns playing the part of the interviewer. Substitute other positions, skills, and work history based on your own experience interviewing for jobs or jobs that you would like to apply for in the future.

3 Read and Think

Step 1. Read the text below.

Joe Martin applied for a job as a cashier at Good Foods grocery store. He was called in for an interview, and when he arrived the receptionist gave him a list of responsibilities and required skills for the cashier position. He read through the list while he was waiting for his interview.

CASHIER

RESPONSIBILITIES/DUTIES:

- Rings up sales of all store items
- Processes customers' payments made in cash, by check, or by credit card
- Packs customers' purchases in bags
- Assists customers with questions
- Other duties as assigned

SKILLS/OTHER REQUIREMENTS:

- Must have good math skills; experience handling money a plus
- Must be able to use hands to work on cash register and handle customers' purchases; some lifting ability
- Must have excellent communication skills
- Must be high school graduate

Step 2. With a partner, read the paragraph below. Circle Joe's job skills and match them to the list of skills required by Good Foods. Do you think Joe is a good candidate for this job?

Joe never worked in a grocery store, but he knew he had some of the skills they were looking for. He was always good in math in school, and he finished secondary school in his native country. He was attending English classes three nights a week and was supposed to move up to the advanced level soon. He once had his own business, so he was experienced with handling money exchanges.

Vocabulary

handle (verb) touch with your hands; work with
item a single unit in a group or list
process (verb) complete all of the steps in a task

responsibilities/duties things an employee is required to do at work
ring up enter a price on a cash register

Step 3. Look at the title of the text below. This is from a job search book Joe found at the library. What do you think the text says? What advice do you think there is?

Step 4. Read the text and think about this question: Which questions is Joe likely to hear in an interview?

How to Handle Difficult Interview Questions

Have you ever had this experience? You go into a job interview, and the interviewer asks you a lot of unusual questions. Many of the questions seem completely unrelated to the job. You try to answer them, but you get the feeling that your answers aren't good enough for the interviewer.

Career counselors say that more and more employers are using psychological techniques in job interviews. Employers are looking for ways to find the negative aspects of a job candidate's personality or work history.

Here are some of the questions employers are asking:
1. What are your strengths?
2. What are your weaknesses?
3. How did you hear about our company?
4. Why did you leave your last job?

When an employer asks about your strengths, you should say positive things. You are a hard worker, you love your work, you loved high school and college, you get along well with your co-workers, etc.

When an employer asks about your weaknesses, don't say anything negative about yourself. Instead, say something that sounds positive, like "Sometimes I work too hard" or "I push myself too hard."

Employers ask the third question to find out a job applicant's knowledge of the company. Learn everything you can about the company before you go into the interview.

Another tough question is why you left your last job. Do not complain about your previous employer, even if the situation at your last job was very bad. Instead, emphasize economic factors such as layoffs, low profit margins, etc.

Step 5. Look at the vocabulary on the next page. Find these words in a dictionary and then read the text again.

Vocabulary

aspects	impression	profit	tough
emphasize	layoffs	psychological	unrelated
factors	margins	techniques	

Step 6. In a group, answer the following questions:

1. What is the main idea of the text on page 39? Is there one sentence that expresses that idea?
2. Can you find one or two strategies for successful job interviews that would be helpful to you? What are they?
3. Why do you think you shouldn't complain about your last job?

Practice

Complete the sentences with the correct words from the vocabulary list on page 39. Be sure to use the correct form of the word or phrase.

1. There were so many _____ *items* _____ on the list I didn't finish reading them all.

2. You must _____ eggs and babies carefully—they're delicate.

3. I don't want any more _____ at work. I have enough to do.

4. It takes about six weeks to get a new driver's license because the Department of Motor

    Vehicles has so many applications to _____.

5. Are there any cashiers around? I need someone to _____ this purchase so I can pay for it.

4 Put It in Writing

Step 1. Think about your current job or a job you had in the past. Write a list of three responsibilities or duties you have or had on that job.

Example: Processed customers' payments

Step 2. Now write a list of three skills required for the same job.

Example: Must have excellent communication skills

5 Listen and Speak

Step 1. Sometimes people don't know how to answer the more unusual questions in a job interview, and sometimes the interview can go badly. Listen to the conversation.

A: Well, you certainly have a number of strong qualities. Now tell me about your weak points.

B: Excuse me? My weak points?

A: Yes. What do you think you need to improve?

B: Oh, well, I don't know. Nothing. I don't have any weak points. I'm good at my work, and I'm highly skilled. But is there a point to this? Am I supposed to say something bad about myself? Like, I always show up late to work or something?

A: Do you always show up late to work?

B: No! I'm always on time. But I don't know how I'm supposed to answer the question.

A: You're just supposed to tell me what you could do better.

B: Well, maybe I could improve my English.

A: Your English is very good. But if you want to improve it, you might want to take some classes at a community college.

B: You think I should take classes? Where?

A: I don't know, but you might take a look at Hadley Community College. They have some good classes there. One of our employees will be taking classes there next semester.

Step 2. Practice the conversation with a partner, and as you do, think about the things that you could change.

Step 3. With another pair of classmates, form a group. Choose a team leader, a team recorder, and a team reporter. Think about these questions: What should the job candidate do differently? What should the job candidate avoid saying? What would be a good response? Brainstorm a number of possible responses to the question "What are your weak points?"

Step 4. Rank your ideas from best to worst. Then choose one of them and create a different conversation, one that ends well.

Step 5. Role-play your conversation within your group. Make any changes you think are necessary.

Step 6. Your team leader and your team reporter will role-play your conversation for the class. Listen to the other group's conversations and evaluate them. Choose the one that is the most successful.

6 Read and Write

Step 1. For each position listed below, read the list of responsibilities and duties.

DRIVER
- Drives customers to and from airport and residences
- Assists passengers with luggage
- Communicates with dispatcher regarding unscheduled pickups

TEACHER
- Teaches all subjects to children in grades 1 and 2
- Prepares lesson plans weekly
- Attends all school planning meetings
- Communicates with parents regarding students' progress

APPLIANCE REPAIR PERSON
- Responds to requests for repairs on major home appliances
- Prepares repair cost estimates for customers
- Travels to residences throughout metropolitan area for repairs
- Maintains inventory of necessary tools and supplies
- Collects payment from customers

Step 2. Write a list of skills that you think would be required to perform each job.

Step 3. Compare your lists of skills with a partner. Do you agree? Add to your list if necessary.

Form and Function

1 I don't know how I'm supposed to answer this question.

I	**am**	**supposed to** answer the question.
you, they, we	**are**	
he, she, it	**is**	

I	**am not**	**supposed to** answer the question.
you, they, we	**are not (aren't)**	
he, she, it	**is not (isn't)**	

What	**am** I	**supposed to** do?
	are we, you, they	
	is he, she, it	

Examples

John **is supposed to** start work at 7:00 this morning. **I'm not supposed to** come in until 8:30. We**'re** all **supposed to** sign this card for Mr. Lopez's birthday.

Practice 1

A. Listen. Circle T or F for True or False.

1. I expect Jill to call me tonight.   (T)   F

2. It's OK if Sam and I take breaks together.   T   F

3. The meeting might start later than 9:00.   T   F

4. Employees' families are invited to the party.   T   F

5. I don't think Maria is going to quit her job.   T   F

B. Think of three things you're supposed to do at your present job or a job you had in the past. Write them below. Then tell a partner.

Example: *I'm supposed to start my shift at 7:30 every morning.*

1. _____

2. _____

3. _____

C. Talk to a partner. What are you supposed to do for your classes? Think of all the things you are supposed to do and discuss them.

2 You might take a look at Hadley Community College. It has a good program.

I, you, he, she, it, we, they	**might** **might not**	**take** a look at it.
I, you, he, she, it, we, they	**might want to** **might not want to**	**take** a look at it. **do** that.

Usage note: *Might* can express a softened recommendation. For the negative form of this kind of recommendation, *might not want to* is most common.

Examples
A: I don't know which ad I should answer.
B: You **might answer** the ad for a computer programmer. That looks like a good job, and it pays well. You **might want** to think about the vocational program at Lang Tech. I've heard good things about it.
A: I'm thinking about taking a job at WonderToys.
B: You **might not want** to do that. I've heard the company is going bankrupt.

Practice 2

A. Listen. Does the speaker recommend the person, place, or thing?

1. recommends	doesn't recommend	4. recommends	doesn't recommend
2. recommends	doesn't recommend	5. recommends	doesn't recommend
3. recommends	doesn't recommend	6. recommends	doesn't recommend

B. Look at the dialogues below. Rewrite the recommendation (the second part of each dialogue) with a sentence with *might*, *might want to*, or *might not want to*.

1. A: I have three good candidates for this job—Fatima, Alicia, and Samantha—and I can't make up my mind. I don't know which one to hire.
   B: I recommend you hire Fatima. I know someone who worked with her. She's good.
   You might want to hire Fatima.

2. A: There's a job opening at AFT Warehouse. I think I might apply for it.
   B: I don't recommend you do that. I've heard safety conditions are bad there.
   _____

3. A: I'm really tired of the low pay I get here. I'm going to ask the boss for a raise.
   B: I don't recommend you do that today. He's in a bad mood.
   _____

4. A: Where's the best office to apply for a driver's license? There are three in the phone book.
   B: I recommend you go to the office in the suburbs. You don't have to wait very long there.
   _____

5. A: I don't know which car I want. All three are good.
   B: I recommend the small car. You'll spend less on gasoline.
   _____

C. Look at the ads below. With a partner, practice recommending the things or the places in the ads. Use any of the expressions you know for recommendations.

COMPUTER DISKS IN BULK

40 DISKS FOR $10.00

THIS WEEK AT TECHWORLD

Computer Disks Name Brands

Box of 15 for $14.99

Till 9/14 at SuperShop

Used textbooks 20% off label price

This week at Johanna's Bookstore on Division Street

SALE!!!
On sofas and armchairs 30% off regular price!!!

Till 9/30 at **The Furniture Mart**

TELEPHONES

Regular: $34.99 and $44.99

Cellular: $59.99 and $79.99

KINGSIZE BEDS

$259.99

This week at
HAROLD HALL FURNITURE

Putting It to Work

Step 1.   Listen. With a partner, complete the list of skills required for each job.

• Must be computer literate

• Must have excellent _____
• Must be able to handle busy phones

• Must be _____
• Must be self-starter
• Must be willing to travel

• _____ strongly desirable

• Must have _____ of audio/video equipment

• Must be _____ nights and weekends

• Must have some restaurant _____
• Outgoing personality a plus

• _____ with numbers

Step 2.   What kinds of jobs are these? With your partner, write a job title by each group of skills. Have either of you ever had any jobs like these? Add any other skills you think would be required for these jobs.

Step 3.   For each of the jobs above, conduct an interview with your partner. Take turns playing the role of the interviewer and applicant.

As an **interviewer**: Remember to ask open-ended questions instead of questions that require only a "yes" or "no" response. Allow the applicant time to answer each question completely. Find out as much information as you can with a few good questions.

As an **applicant**: Think about your answers before you respond to questions. Remember to smile and make eye contact. Be sure to give the interviewer as much information about your job skills as possible.

Step 4.   Once you have conducted each interview, ask another pair of classmates to watch one of your interviews and critique you. Ask them to make suggestions for ways you can improve your interviewing techniques. Then watch them conduct one of their interviews and critique them.

2 Group/Class Work

Step 1. In a group, choose any occupation you all know. Work together to come up with a list of responsibilities/duties and job skills required for the job.

Step 2. Write the job description including all of the information from Step 1.

Step 3. Now work together to write a list of interview questions to find someone for that position.

Step 4. Choose an interviewer or committee from your group to conduct the interviews. You must interview each applicant for the position by asking the same questions in the same order.

Step 5. Choose two people from the group to be interviewed. Both applicants are equally qualified for the position, but one will use excellent interviewing skills; the other will not be quite as skilled. With the group, plan your answers to the questions and the behavior to be used by each applicant during the interviews.

Step 6. Conduct your interviews in front of the class. After both interviews have been done, allow the class to critique each applicant's interviewing skills.

3 Culture Work

Step 1. Read the two conversations below. The first is between Al and Paulo, who are friends. The second is between Paulo and the personnel manager of a large company. Paulo didn't know how to speak to the personnel manager, so he didn't get the job. Why not?

Al: Hey, Paulo! How's it going, man?
Paulo: Al! All right! How's it going with you?
Al: Nothing to complain about, I guess.
Paulo: Hey, guess what? I have a job interview right now.
Al: Hey, that's fantastic, Paulo. Hope it goes well. See you.
Paulo: Yeah, thanks, see you.

Personnel Manager: Hello, I'm Martin Burtin.
Paulo: Hey, Martin, I'm Paulo. How's it going?
Personnel Manager: Fine. Have a seat.
Paulo: Fantastic! Nice place here!
Personnel Manager: Did you bring your résumé?
Paulo: Yeah, sure. Here it is.
Personnel Manager: How long have you been in the United States?
Paulo: Three years. And it's been a good time.

Step 2. Paulo spoke too informally with the personnel manager. With the class, discuss these questions:

How should Paulo have said things differently?
What shouldn't Paulo have said in the interview?
What changes would you suggest for Paulo?
When do you speak formally, and when do you speak informally?

Openers

Look at the picture. How do the words below apply?

pay envelope   benefits   sick days

Where is Ali? What do you think happened? Have you ever been in a situation like this?

1 Listen and Think

Listen to the conversation. Then answer the questions with a partner.

1. How often does Ali receive his paycheck?

2. Does he have any sick days left?

3. Who writes down the hours that each worker works and takes off?

2 Talk to a Partner

Step 1. Practice the conversation with a partner.

A: Sonia, excuse me. Have you got a second?

B: What is it, Rashida?

A: Um, I think my check is wrong.

B: Do you have the stub?

A: Yeah, here, look. Remember? I worked 14 hours overtime in the last two weeks, not 12. My paycheck says only 12.

B: OK. I'll have to take a look at the time card.

A: Do you want me to go to the office?

B: No, no. I'll take care of it.

A: OK. Let me know, all right?

B: Sure. See you later.

A: Thanks, Sonia.

B: Sure thing, Rashida.

Step 2. With a partner, role-play a similar situation. What do you do if there is an error in your paycheck? Who can you talk to?

3 Read and Think

Step 1. Before you read, make a list of the payroll deductions that are detailed on your paycheck stub. Compare your list with that of a partner.

Step 2. Read this section from the Acme Manufacturing Company's Employee Handbook.

Payroll Deductions

By law, Acme Manufacturing must deduct four taxes from your paycheck: (1) federal income tax, (2) state income tax, (3) Social Security tax, and (4) Medicare tax. The amount of income tax deducted depends on your earnings and the number of allowances you claim on your W-4 Form each year.

These amounts go to the U.S. and state treasuries. The company provides a record of these deductions at the end of each year. This is your W-2 Form.

The company will withhold other deductions from your paycheck if you authorize them in writing. These deductions include, for example, insurance premiums, retirement savings contributions, and uniform fees. On your behalf, the company remits these deductions to the proper agencies.

You should retain your check stubs as a personal record of your earnings and deductions. Notify the Payroll Office immediately if you think there is any error.

Vocabulary

premiums scheduled payments that you make for insurance

remit (to) pay money to another party, for a bill or other regular payment

retain (to) keep, hold on to, not throw away

treasury the place where a government keeps its money

withholding tax money taken out of one's pay

Step 3. Before you read the chart below, answer these pre-reading questions:

1. Do you work for a private company or a public (government) organization?

2. Do you work full-time (that is, an average of 30 hours or more per week at one job)?

3. Which one of your benefits is the most important to you?

Step 4. Read the chart below and then answer the questions.

Percentage of U.S. Civilian Workers Whose Employers Offer Selected Types of Benefits (May 1988)

BENEFIT	NUMBER OF WORKERS		SICK LEAVE		HEALTH INSURANCE		DISABILITY INSURANCE	
Employer	Private	Public	Private	Public	Private	Public	Private	Public
TOTAL	84.7 million	17.1 m.	52%	83%	75%	93%	36%	49%
Full-Time	71.2 m.	15.0 m.	59%	90%	81%	95%	41%	55%
Part-Time	13.5 m.	2.1 m.	15%	32%	46%	80%	8%	13%

SOURCE OF DATA: The Employee Benefits Research Institute

Questions: **1.** Which benefit type is most common for full-time workers in private companies?
      a. Sick Leave   **b.** Health Insurance   **c.** Disability Insurance

      2. How many workers in private companies in 1988 did not have paid sick leave?
      a. 84.7 million   **b.** 17.1 million   **c.** 40.7 million

Step 5. Look again at the list of benefits that you wrote in Step 1 on page 50. Then look at the longer list below. Check off the benefits that you receive in your present job.

Paid Time Not Working
____ Holidays
____ Vacation Days
____ Lunch or Rest Period
____ Funeral Leave
____ Sick Leave

Other Benefits
____ Health Insurance (for you)
____ Health Insurance (for your dependents)
____ Life Insurance
____ Disability Insurance
____ Retirement Benefits (paid by the company)

Vocabulary

civilian not military

disability the inability to work; the condition/reason why one cannot work

duration length of time

extended longer or larger than usual

funeral special ceremony for the dead

initiative first move or step; the power to make the first step

jury duty when a person goes to court to help decide a case (U.S. culture)

offer (to) make available, give, if desired

period (lunch, rest) an amount of time to do something

plan (benefits) an arrangement, in advance, for doing something

retirement a time when older people stop doing work for pay; payments to live on during this time

Worker's Compensation payment that workers get if they are injured on the job

4 Put It in Writing

Step 1. Answer the questions below.

1. If you are employed, what kinds of benefits do you have? Describe your benefits in a few sentences.

   _____

   _____

   _____

2. If you are unemployed, what kinds of benefits are you looking for?

   _____

   _____

   _____

3. Do you have (or do you need) health insurance for yourself only, for yourself and your spouse, or for yourself and your entire family?

   _____

   _____

   _____

Step 2. With a partner, compare your work.

5 Listen and Speak

Step 1. **Two employees are talking about benefits. Listen to the conversation.**

A: I used to work at a company that gave everyone two weeks of vacation the first year.

B: Really? That's great. That's much better than here.

A: Yeah, and we had more holidays, too. We had Washington's Birthday and Lincoln's Birthday off.

B: What kind of place was that, a bank?

A: No, it was a manufacturing company, like this one.

B: Well, why did you leave that place?

A: I'm making more money here. And actually, except for the vacations, the benefits are better here.

B: Really? What kinds of benefits did you get there?

A: Well, the dental coverage was as good as the coverage here, but the health plan wasn't as comprehensive. We paid more money, and the plan covered less.

B: Yeah, well, the premiums are going up here, too. Betty said the company planned to change insurance companies. And the new plans are more expensive because the company isn't going to pay as much as before.

A: Will we still be able to choose our own doctor? Or will we have to pick one from a list?

B: Well, Betty said it was an HMO, so you probably won't be able to go to your own doctor.

A: I don't like that idea. I've been going to my doctor for 20 years. He knows me really well. Why should I change now?

B: Listen, you ought to talk to Betty about it. She has more information than I do.

Step 2. **Practice the conversation with a partner.**

Step 3. **Create a second part to the conversation above. Look at the information below about the new health and dental plans. Role-play a conversation with the personnel manager. Which benefits are most important to you? Discuss the question with your partner. Note: With the HMO, you have to choose one of the HMO doctors.**

Health: 2 Possible Plans

Traditional Plan
Cost: $150.00 a month
           $300.00 deductible
Coverage: 80% of all hospitalization costs
           100% of basic doctor visits

HMO
Cost: $57.00 a month
           $20.00 payment per visit
Coverage: 95% of hospitalization*
           100% of basic doctor visits

*Hospitalization is subject to approval.

Dental: 2 Plans

Traditional Plan
Cost: $50.00 a month
           $200.00 deductible
Coverage: 85% of routine work
           60% of major dental work

HMO
Cost: $35.00 a month
           $20.00 payment per visit
           100% of routine work
           75% of major dental work*

*See list of major dental work.

---

6 Read and Write

Step 1.   Read the summary of employee benefits for Acme employees.

Summary of Employee Benefits

Benefit	Description	Eligible Employees		
		FULL-TIME	TEMPORARY	PART-TIME
A. TIME OFF WITH REGULAR PAY				
1. Holidays	Nine days per year.	X	X	X
2. Sick Leave	5/6th of a day per month of employment after first 60 days. Cumulative if not used.	X		
3. Funeral Leave	Up to 3 days for loss of a member of one's immediate family. 1 day for other relatives.	X		X
4. Vacation	After 12 months, 10 days. 15 days after the third year of continuous employment. Prior approval required.	X		
5. Personal Days	After 4 months, 2 days per year. Prior approval required.	X		
B. TIME OFF WITHOUT PAY				
6. Medical or Disability Leave	After sick leave is used up. Up to 6 months.	X		
7. Dependent Care	Up to 6 months. Certain restrictions apply.	X		X
C. INSURANCE				
8. Health Plan	After 60 days of employment. Company pays 50% of employee's coverage, if selected.	X		
9. Disability	Basic Plan: Acme pays premiums. For optional Extended Plan: Employee pays premiums.	X		
10. Worker's Compensation	Government plan. Company pays premiums. For disability due to injury on the job.	X	X	X
11. Dental/Vision Group Plan	Optional. Employee pays premiums.	X		

Step 2.   Now write three questions and answers about Acme's employee benefits.

> **Example:** How long must an employee work before he or she gets a paid vacation? (Answer: 12 months.)

Step 3.   With a partner, compare your work and discuss your questions.

Form and Function

1 The dental coverage at that company was as good as the coverage here.

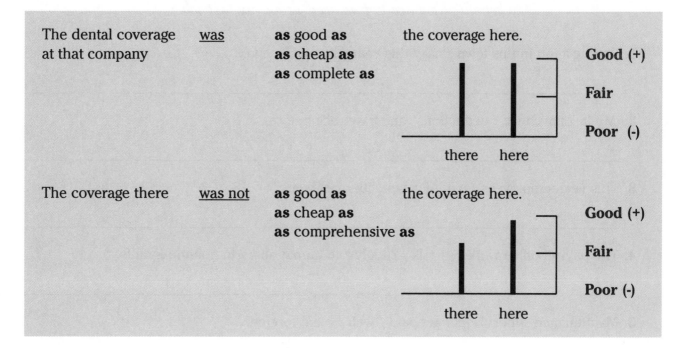

The dental coverage at that company <u>was</u> **as** good **as** / **as** cheap **as** / **as** complete **as** the coverage here.

Good (+) / Fair / Poor (−)
there   here

The coverage there <u>was not</u> **as** good **as** / **as** cheap **as** / **as** comprehensive **as** the coverage here.

Good (+) / Fair / Poor (−)
there   here

Examples

Employers are not hiring **as many** immigrants **as** before.

Tom punched in **as soon as** he arrived.

Production workers with five or more years of employment get **as many** vacation days **as** office workers get after only three years.

Practice 1

A. Listen to the news report on employee benefits in the United States. Then listen again and answer the questions. Mark T or F for True or False.

1. Employment has increased this year.   T   Ⓕ

2. Business profits increased less than last year.   T   F

3. The cost of employee benefits is lower than before.   T   F

4. Health-care costs are increasing faster than inflation is. T   F

B. Combine each group of phrases to make a complete sentence expressing a comparison. Add words that you need. Use *as . . . as* wherever possible.

> **Example:** My benefits now / good / on my last job.
>
> *My benefits now are not as good as on my last job.*

1. Getting a job in this town / easy this year / five years ago.

_____

2. My last paycheck / deductions / the paycheck before.

_____

3. This year, employees / pay / for benefits / last year.

_____

4. The payroll office workers / talk / rudely / to immigrants / to nonimmigrants.

_____

5. Maintenance supervisors / get paid / well / plant foremen.

_____

C. Read this list of topics. Then write three or more comparative sentences. *Your choice:* Write one sentence each about three topics or three sentences about one topic.

Topics:	Selecting an HMO	Using credit unions
	Taxes	Immigration
	Changing jobs	Benefits for dependents

Examples:

It's not as easy to change jobs as it used to be.

The new job may not pay as much as the old one.

If the pay is better, the benefits may not be as good.

2 Betty said it was an HMO.

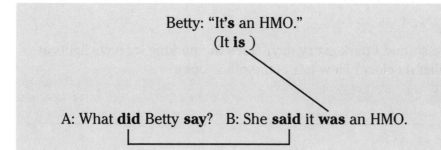

Betty: "It's an HMO."
(It **is**)

A: What **did** Betty **say**?   B: She **said** it **was** an HMO.

"We have a health-care plan.
It's an HMO."

"She said it was an HMO."

Examples

"What's the matter?"   She **asked** me what the matter **was**.
"I don't feel well."   I **told** her (that) I **didn't feel** well.
"We'll count it as a half day sick."   She **said** they **would count** it a half day sick.
"They counted one extra sick day."   I **pointed** out that they **counted** one extra sick day.

Practice 2

A. Read the sentences. Listen to the story and put the sentences in order. Write the number next to the corresponding sentence.

____ He said he didn't have a lot of time.   ____ He asked what the problem was.

____ He asked him to wait a minute.   ____ He said that he was within his rights.

_1_ He said he needed some help.   ____ He said he had work to do, too.

B. Imagine a new second-shift worker asked you the questions below. Rewrite them, starting with "She said that she had a few questions." Then report the questions to a partner in class.

I have a few questions. Where should I park every day? Does the parking lot have lights at night? What time does the cafeteria close? How late is the office open?

1. _____

2. _____

3. _____

4. _____

5. _____

C. With a partner, look at the pictures and captions below. Talk about what each person said.

"You owe me another five dollars!"

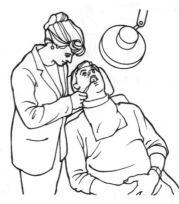

"Your teeth look very good."

"Where's the wrench?

"How's Mrs. Johnson?"

D. Think about some of the things your employer or your teacher said last week. Tell your partner.

Putting It to Work

1 Pair Work

Step 1. In pairs, decide which partner will listen and write and which one will read the information presented. All *readers* must leave the room. All *listeners* stay in their seats.

Step 2. *Listeners* (in classroom): Listen to the recording of the personnel officer from Acme Manufacturing. Take dictation. Write down the five sentences he says. Check your answers with the other *listeners*.

Readers (in other room or hallway): Reread the Summary of Employee Benefits on page 54. Make sure you understand. Check your comprehension with other Readers.

Step 3. In pairs again, *listeners* report what the Acme personnel officer said. Read your dictation to your partner. Everyone should know that the Acme personnel officer made some mistakes in what he said. *Readers* should look in the Summary to find the correct information.

Example: L: The personnel guy said that part-timers do not get any time off with pay.
R: But it says here that part-timers are eligible for paid funeral leave and . . .

2 Pair Work

Step 1. Change partners. Discuss what you like and do not like about the package of employee benefits at the company where you work. If you are not working now, talk about Acme Manufacturing's benefits or the benefits you had at a previous job.

Step 2. List the advantages and disadvantages of the benefits package under pros (advantages) and cons (disadvantages).

Pros	Cons

Step 3. With another pair of classmates, compare what you have written. Compare your benefits packages and the pros and cons of each.

3 Group/Class Work

Step 1.   Form groups of four to six students. Each person should write down the three employee benefits that are most important to you.

Step 2.   Select a group reporter. He or she will write down on one piece of paper a list of the "Most Important Benefits" that are named by the group.

Step 3.   Discuss the list. Ask each other questions, or defend your choices. Then vote as a group on the top three most important benefits for your group. You can only have three from your group, so keep talking and debating until you agree on the three most important.

Step 4.   The reporter for each group then presents the group's top three benefits to the class. Each reporter should write his or her top three on the blackboard, and discuss why these are the most important. Other group members may help the reporter.

4 Culture Work

A national survey of employers in all types of private companies and in local and state government units provided the information below. Read and discuss this chart in class. Compare the benefits in different types and sizes of companies in the United States, and with employee benefits that you know about in other countries.

Employee Benefit Program Participation By Full-Time Employees, 1989–1990			
Private Establishments			
	Small Companies *less than 100 workers*	**Medium and Large Companies** *100 workers or more*	**State and Local Governments**
EMPLOYEE BENEFIT PROGRAM			
Health Insurance (total)	**69%**	**92%**	**93%**
For employee:			
Wholly Employer Financed	40%	48%	58%
Partly Employer Financed	29%	44%	35%
For employee's family:			
Wholly Employer Financed	22%	31%	32%
Partly Employer Financed	46%	60%	60%
Life Insurance (total)	**64%**	**94%**	**88%**
For employee:			
Wholly Employer Financed	53%	82%	77%
Partly Employer Financed	11%	12%	11%
Retirement (all types that are financed wholly or partly by the employer)	42%	81%	96%

Unit 6
JOB DESCRIPTIONS AND DUTIES

Openers

Look at the picture. How do the words below apply to the situation you see?

job grade   duties   organization   benefits

Where is Alberto? What is he doing? Have you seen your job description?
Who would you ask at your company to get it from? Have you ever seen your
company's organization chart?

1 Listen and Think

Listen and answer the questions with a partner.

1. How many main departments are in this company?

2. Are "Shipping" and "Delivery" the same area or different areas of the company?

3. Had Alberto met his foreman before this conversation took place?

4. Where will Alberto go next?

2 Talk to a Partner

Step 1. Shipping foreman Margaret Fox is completing new van driver Alberto Mendez's orientation to his work area and job duties. Practice the conversation with a partner.

A: OK, Alberto, you pick up your orders here at the desk. Then what?

B: I follow the routing and make sure that I load the boxes for the last delivery stop into the van first.

A: Right. And the orders?

B: I check off the items on all the orders to make sure I have them in the truck before I leave.

A: Good, good. And you put the pink copies . . .?

B: In the "out" box. Stapled together.

A: And what's the last step?

B: I write down the time I leave. And I go.

A: You've got it. You're off to a great start. Now just do it like you said.

B: OK. I sure will.

Step 2. With your partner, talk about a work routine you know.

Step 3. Role-play a similar conversation.

3 Read and Think

Step 1. Read this job description format. Draw lines from the categories to the eight parts of a job description.

POSITION DESCRIPTION (FORMAT)

JOB TITLE:	The name of the position
UNIT:	Name of department, division, or section
REPORTS TO:	Supervisor's title
SUMMARY:	A short statement about the purpose of the job within the company.
DUTIES AND RESPONSIBILITIES:	Statements about the specific tasks, duties, or responsibilities.
Major Duties	The most important and biggest parts of the job.
Minor Duties	Those that are less important or less common.
QUALIFICATIONS:	A description of the skills or knowledge required; educational background; amount of experience; training, licenses, or certificates needed, etc. May include aptitude (such as mechanical, mathematical, verbal, problem-solving, and organizing abilities).
INTERRELATIONSHIPS:	(Not in all job descriptions) A statement that describes the other people this person interacts with, both within and outside of the company. If this person supervises other workers, specify here.
WORKING CONDITIONS:	A description of the usual physical conditions of work in this position: time; travel; exposure to the elements; requirements for strength, lifting, standing, sitting, vision; safety and health considerations, etc.

Vocabulary

aptitude the talent or ability to do something, whether or not one has experience doing it

the elements the weather, including wind, temperature, rain/snow, etc.

exposure being uncovered, in the open, or in contact with something

format the usual organization and look that a document has or should have

interrelationships relationships between people; how people get along together

"out" box the place on a desk or wall to put paperwork that one has finished and which then goes to another worker (to the "in" box)

physical referring to muscles, places, or other nonmental things or aspects

purpose the reason for something

routing the steps or schedule of where to go or where to send something

staple (to) attach together with a special machine (a stapler) and bent metal wires (staples)

task an assignment; an action to perform

training special study, courses, practice, or other learning that is related to a job, especially when the job is new

Step 2. Now read part of Alberto Mendez's delivery van driver job description.

(Name of section)

Must have valid truck operator's license for the state.
Three years' experience driving small trucks or similar vehicles.
No traffic violations in the past two years.
Very good knowledge of area streets and highways.
Ability to interact with customers in a positive manner.
Able to lift up to 75 pounds.
High school completion or equivalent preferred.

Step 3. Refer to the Position Description format and write the correct name for this section of the job description into the box above.

Step 4. Read this chart describing the operational processes in Alberto's company.

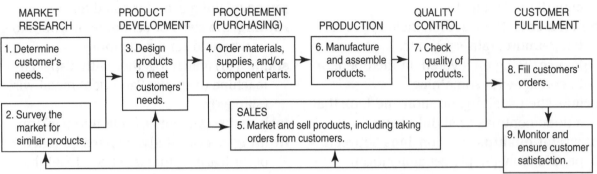

SEQUIN-TURNER CORPORATION
MAJOR OPERATIONS CONTROL CHART

MARKET RESEARCH	PRODUCT DEVELOPMENT	PROCUREMENT (PURCHASING)	PRODUCTION	QUALITY CONTROL	CUSTOMER FULFILLMENT

1. Determine customer's needs.
2. Survey the market for similar products.
3. Design products to meet customers' needs.
4. Order materials, supplies, and/or component parts.
SALES
5. Market and sell products, including taking orders from customers.
6. Manufacture and assemble products.
7. Check quality of products.
8. Fill customers' orders.
9. Monitor and ensure customer satisfaction.

Answer the questions below. Write the number from the Major Operations Control Chart on the blank.

Which major operation includes:

____ a. shipping and delivery to customers?

____ b. receiving raw materials?

____ c. checking for product quality before shipping?

____ d. monitoring customer complaints after shipping?

____ e. taking customers' orders?

____ f. developing new products?

____ g. producing products for customers?

Step 5. Referring to the chart again, write the number of the most appropriate operation for these job titles.

____ h. Foreman, Electrical Assembly

____ i. Telemarketing Associate

____ j. Quality Control Analyst

____ k. Receiving Inventory Clerk

____ l. Delivery Driver

____ m. Sales Manager

____ n. Assembler

____ o. Packer/Shipper

____ p. Customer Assistant

____ q. Materials Buyer

Vocabulary

components the parts that make up a whole

equivalent the same as, equal to (in value)

fulfill (to) meet a need (fulfillment)

inventory the type and quantity of products or materials that one has; the counting of such stuff, as in inventory

market (n) the state of trade for certain goods; (to) bring to market, sell, offer for sale

monitor (to) watch over, attend to, keep track of and report on an activity

procurement obtaining what is needed; (to) procure

telemarketing selling by telephone

valid good, legal, currently in effect

vehicles cars, trucks, buses, motorcycles, etc.

violations errors, mistakes recorded by the police, courts, or other authorities

4 Put It in Writing

Step 1. Answer the questions below about your present job. If necessary, get this information from your co-workers or your boss. If you do not have a job now, answer for a job you are familiar with (a former job or a friend or family member's job).

1. What is the name of your position? _____

   Example: *Team Leader*

2. What department, division, or other unit is your job located in? _____

3. What is your supervisor's position? _____

Step 2. Write five or more phrases that describe the most important and most frequent duties you perform on your job. Then write a general statement or summary of your job. You can use the pairs of verbs and nouns in the Word Bank below as a guide to describing some types of job duties. Of course, as you write, you may also use your dictionary and talk to classmates, teacher, and other resources.

JOB DUTIES WORD BANK

Verbs	Nouns	Verbs	Nouns
Operate	machine	Sort	materials
Maintain	machinery	Handle	supplies
Inspect	(type of) equipment	Pack	(type of) orders
Set up	vehicle	Inventory	parts
Clean	parts	Route	paperwork
Repair	equipment	Organize	shipments
Complete	documents	Perform	duties
Fill out	(type of) orders	Complete	(type of) tasks
Prepare	reports	Supervise	(type of) process

Example: Duties: Keep track of all parts received. Complete required paperwork.
Route parts to different departments.
Operate forklift. Inspect it daily.
Keep receiving dock clean.
Supervise other materials handlers on the shift.

Summary: Responsible for receiving parts and routing them internally.

Step 3. With a partner, read each other's job descriptions. Comment on your partner's work and ask questions about anything that seems unclear. Make at least one suggestion to your partner about his/her work. Revise your job description and/or organization chart based on your partner's feedback.

5 Listen and Speak

Step 1. An administrative assistant is explaining a job to a new employee. Listen to the conversation.

A: I'll just describe the job briefly. As you know, your job title will be administrative assistant for the director of operations, so you will do the work that Ms. Martinez assigns to you. That's the job that I had had before.

B: Could you describe the work that I'm supposed to do?

A: Sure. Typically, you organize Ms. Martinez's correspondence—all of the letters and other mail that she receives—that could be E-mail, for example, or faxes. You maintain Ms. Martinez's files, and you set up her appointments. You talk to people who want to talk to Ms. Martinez, and if a person is someone that Ms. Martinez doesn't want to talk to, you don't let that person through.

B: Oh. I see. That's important.

A: Of course. Now let's look at the filing system. Here's a contract. Contracts are documents that go into the drawers that say "Legal." You put contracts in the front section, and you file them by the company name that you see on the front. Understand?

B: Sure. So far, so good.

A: OK, great. Well, I had wanted to talk about the computer system, but it's already time to go.

Step 2. With a partner, practice the conversation.

Step 3. Role-play a similar conversation between two employees. Describe a job you know.

6 Read and Write

Step 1. Transfer the information about your job duties from the job description you wrote on page 67 to the form below. You may add more if you would like.

Job Title:		Date:	
Duties or Activities	Priority	Time Spent	Ideal Time
	Totals	100%	100%

Step 2. Use the form to consider key aspects of job duties, such as (1) the importance of an activity, (2) the time needed to complete an activity, and (3) the time available to complete assigned work.

Step 3. With a partner, compare your work.

Form and Function

1 Contracts are documents that go into those drawers.

Ask questions about anything.   Ask questions about <u>anything</u> **that** is not clear.
Something is not clear.   **which**

Examples

Here is some key <u>information</u> **which** you will need on the job.
Every <u>customer</u> **that** you speak to is important to our business.
The <u>service</u> **which** you give to our customers determines the future of our company and our jobs.

Practice 1

A. Listen to each pair of short sentences. Then read the longer combined sentences below. Underline the connecting word (*that* or *which*).

1. At times, customers will make requests that may seem impossible to meet.

2. For example, they may have a deadline that we might not be able to meet.

3. Ali has a job description that lists all of his responsibilities.

4. Greta has a job that pays very well.

5. In our office, we have photocpiers that are very old.

B. Using the clauses below, combine the groups of sentences using *that* or *which*.

1. Our company follows an approach to work [   ].

This approach to work encourages innovation.

2. Each operation is assigned to a work team [   ].

The work team is responsible for carrying out the operation.

3. The work team organizes itself in the way [   ].

They think this way is most efficient.

4. Most of the positive changes [   ] have been designed by the work teams.

These positive changes have occurred in the past two years.

5. And the company rewards the work teams [   ] [   ].

These work teams have come up with processes [   ].

These processes improve productivity and efficiency.

C. Rewrite the following questions without *that* or *that is / are*.

1. What is the single most important duty that you perform in your present position?

2. Are you usually able to complete all your duties in the time that is allotted?

3. What are the most important skills or qualifications that are required for successful performance?

4. List all the tools, equipment, and machinery that are used to carry out the duties of this job.

5. Are there any "secrets" or "tricks" to your job that your supervisor doesn't know about?

D. Practice combining each group of sentences in three or more ways. Use *that* or *which* to combine the sentences. Change words like *the*, *a*, *this*, or *these* as needed. Then share your answers with a partner.

1. This is the position.
   I applied for this position.
   This position has several important duties.
   The duties must be performed carefully.
   The duties are described in detail in your new employee packet.
   You received the new employee packet when you started.

2. Every day I make sure that I have the materials/tools/supplies.

I need materials/tools/supplies to do the job.

The job is on the work order.

The work order lists the materials/tools/supplies.

I report for work every day.

E. With a partner, talk about your own jobs or a job you know. First describe the job. Then tell each other the steps that you need to follow for a specific job duty.

2 That's the job that I had done before.

1	**2**
I <u>did</u> that job.	Then I <u>got</u> a different job.

I **had done** that job **before** I **got** a different one.

Examples

Before I came to the United States, I **had worked** in my profession for twelve years. By the time I was promoted to a supervisory position in this country, I **had had** five more years of work experience.

Practice 2

A. Listen to these two-clause sentences. Mark the flow of time in each.

Mark	**A B**	if A had occurred before B took place;
	B A	if B had occurred before A took place.

	A	B
A B	**1.** When Mario had finished	he reported to his boss.
_____	**2.** By the time the job was over	Mohammed had shipped more than 140 cases.
_____	**3.** Tasha applied again at the very first company	that she had worked at in America.
_____	**4.** Halina found a position doing the same work	that she had done in Poland.
_____	**5.** Zoran had worked there for eight months	before anyone gave him a job description.

B. **Read the sentences below. Then write a longer sentence for the situation. Use the past perfect with *had* to describe what happened first.**

1. I left the house on time. I got to the bus stop. But the bus was down the street already.

   By the time I _____ *got to the bus stop, the bus had already left.* _____.

2. I got to work ten minutes late. Everyone already started working.

   By the time I _____.

3. I started to do my work. My supervisor already noticed I was late.

   By the time I _____.

4. I apologized when I saw her. My supervisor already turned in a report and docked me.

   By the time I _____.

5. The day before, my supervisor wrote up a report. She said I was a good worker.

   Luckily, the day before, _____.

C. Write about the situation below.

Situation: Responding to a Bad Performance Review

The company hired Oscar as a driver on October 15th of last year. On December 10th, they started his training. That was after he had already gone out on the road. A few problems had occurred in late October and in early November. The training eventually included information that Oscar could have used to avoid the earlier problems. Now his performance review includes some negative comments about those problems he had had before his training.

Help Oscar write a response to his bad performance review. Include statements (1) about how long he had worked before his training started, (2) that his only problems had occurred before training, (3) that there were no problems after training, and (4) that he would like the review to take these facts into account.

Putting It to Work

1 Pair Work

Step 1. With a partner, listen as Rosa Vasquez, a Quality Control worker at Seguin-Turner, completes the Job Analysis Questionnaire that her supervisor gave her.

EMPLOYEE JOB ANALYSIS QUESTIONNAIRE

EMPLOYEE   DATE
POSITION   DEPARTMENT
INSTRUCTIONS: Complete this page. Describe in detail the most important duties that you perform on your job. Include all information requested. Questions should be addressed to your Supervisor.

Duty 1. (what)
Procedure (how)
Reason (why)
Frequency (how often)   per hour / day / week / month /
Percentage of work time you spend on this duty: %

Duty 2. (what)

Step 2. With your partner, do you agree about what you heard?

Step 3. Describe two important duties you perform on your job. Refer to the form above as an outline.

2 Pair Work

Preparation: Bring three copies of your job description to class.

Step 1. Write your name and your position title below. Make a class list.

Name	Position Title
Rashida	Order Picker

Step 2. Select a partner whose job description you would like to discuss and, if possible, who would like to discuss yours, too. Get together, exchange job descriptions, and talk about the job, how hard or easy it is, whether or not the job description is accurate and complete, and how you might change the job description to make it more accurate.

3 Group/Class Work

Step 1. Answer the questions to this survey individually. Then add up your answers.

How Do You Use Your Time?

	Always	Sometimes	Never
1. I start my workday by reviewing my assignments and mentally planning my day.	2	1	0
2. Distractions and socializing keep me from concentrating on my work.	2	1	0
3. I have a good system on my job for taking care of paperwork efficiently.	2	1	0
4. My work area is kind of messy and should be neater.	2	1	0
5. I look for ways to improve my work performance.	2	1	0
6. I worry about making the right decision at work.	2	1	0

SCORE: A. Questions 1 + 3 + 5 = _____

B. Questions 2 + 4 + 6 = _____

Subtract line B from line A

TOTAL:

Step 2. The class will divide up into two groups according to the score on your test. If your total score is 3 or more than 3, go to Group 1. If your total score is less than 3, go to Group 2.

Step 3. Discuss your answers in your groups.

Step 4. Discuss the questions below. Make a list of your group's thoughts to share with the class later.

Group 1: What do you think about workers who waste their time? Do you think that any problems they have at work are usually of their own making or their own fault?

Group 2: What do you think of workers who always seem to be right about everything and who seem to do everything right? Do they spoil life at work for other people?

Step 5. Report your ideas to the class.

4 Culture Work

Step 1. Read the information below about attitudes toward work in the United States. Discuss these attitudes with your class.

Workplace Attitudes in the United States

Attitudes	Possible effects of these attitudes
People can influence the future and change or improve their lives.	Each position may affect others. Each job has a specific function.
People should not waste time; they should work quickly and efficiently.	Companies sometimes lay off employees even when there aren't enough people to do all of the work.
A company has a right to fire an employee if he or she doesn't do a good job.	Employers care more about success and productivity than about an employee's loss of a job or resulting financial problems.

Step 2. With your class, discuss any other attitudes toward work in the United States that you know about.

Step 3. Tell the class about attitudes toward work in your native country. How are these attitudes different?

Unit 7
JOB SAFETY PROCEDURES

Openers

Look at the pictures. Identify these things:

a fire extinguisher   a safety sign   a warning indicator   a fire alarm

Have you seen any of these things at your workplace? Do you have any of these things in your home? How are they helpful?

1 Listen and Think

Listen. Then answer the questions with a partner.

1. How does Mario know there's a problem with the machine?

2. Does Mario know what to do about the problem?

3. What does Yelena think Mario should do about the problem?

4. Does Mario think Yelena's suggestion is a good one? Why or why not?

5. What does Yelena think will happen if Mario keeps working on the machine?

2 Talk to a Partner

Step 1. Practice the conversation with a partner.

A: Hey, watch out for those loose wires.
B: Oh, thanks. I didn't see them there.
A: That's really dangerous. I hadn't noticed them either
   until I walked by here this morning.
B: Did you report it to anyone?
A: Yeah, I called maintenance, but no one was there, so
   I just left a message on their voice mail.
B: You know, this could cause a serious accident.
   Why don't we tell Rita about this? She'll take care of it.
A: OK, I guess you're right. It is pretty dangerous, and we should do
   something before it's too late.

Step 2. Now with the same partner, change the conversation to discuss different safety problems. Look at the pictures here or think of some other problems.

Step 3. Role-play a similar conversation about one of the safety problems you have chosen. In your conversation, talk about the cause of the problem and suggest a solution.

3 Read and Think

Step 1. Read the text below.

Teresa went to an employee meeting yesterday. They discussed evacuation procedures in case of a fire or other disaster. They showed a drawing of the company's evacuation plan.

   Some of the information on the drawing included: (**1.**) locations of exits (**2.**) locations of stairways (**3.**) shortest exit routes from different locations within the building.

   The managers said it was every employee's responsibility to know the evacuation route from his or her work area. They said copies of the evacuation plan were posted in every department.

Vocabulary

disaster a large, very dangerous occurrence that usually affects a high number of people (such as fire, tornado, earthquake, hurricane, etc.)

evacuation procedures a series of instructions to follow for leaving a building or other location

fire escape usually a ladder or stairway outside a building that allows someone to exit from an upstairs window

route a way or direction to travel from one location to another

Step 2. With a partner, look at the floor plan for Julia's company and find the exits, stairways, and elevators.

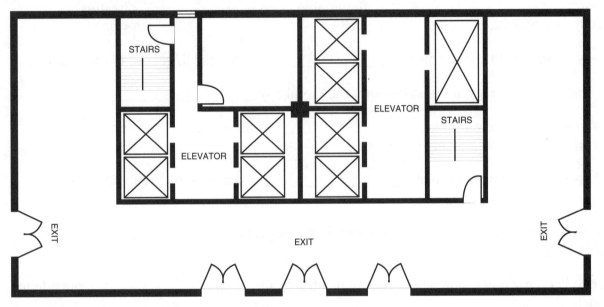

Step 3. Match the following safety signs/symbols with the word(s) that describe them.

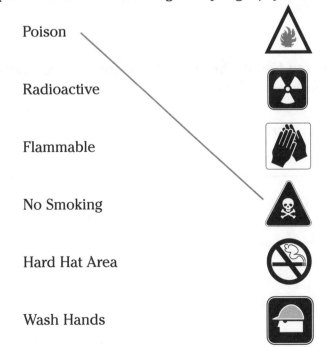

Poison

Radioactive

Flammable

No Smoking

Hard Hat Area

Wash Hands

Vocabulary

flammable able to ignite and burn; also combustible

hard hat a protective helmet worn in areas where there is danger of falling objects

poison a general term for any substance that is harmful to living things

radioactive capable of nuclear reaction

Practice

Complete the sentences with the correct words.

fire escape
evacuation procedures

flammable
route

disasters
poison

1. It's very important to know which _____ *route* _____ to take to get out of the building.

2. Don't leave any oily rags in the storeroom; they're highly _____.

3. Our supervisors reviewed the _____ with us so that everyone would know what to do in case of an emergency.

4. Los Angeles experienced several _____ last year, including brush fires, earthquakes, and mud slides.

5. If you're upstairs when a fire breaks out, see if you can get to a _____ in order to get out.

6. I have to keep my dog inside whenever my neighbor puts _____ outside to kill mice.

4 Put It in Writing

Step 1. Think of your present job or a job you had in the past. Write down three safety procedures you have to or had to follow on the job.

Example: *I have to unplug the equipment before I clean it.*

1. _____

2. _____

3. _____

Step 2. Now write down reasons for following each of the safety procedures on page 78.

Example: *It is dangerous to clean the equipment while it is plugged in.*

1. _____

2. _____

3. _____

5 Listen and Speak

Step 1. Ali isn't sure about something, so he asks for help. But there's a problem. Listen to the conversation.

> Ali: Hey, Gordon, how do you run this press?
> Gordon: Why are *you* running it? Isn't that Paul's job?
> Ali: He called in sick today, so I'm supposed to run it, but I've never done it before.
> Gordon: Well, it looks pretty simple. I think you just lower that lever and hold it for a couple of seconds.

Step 2. Practice the conversation with a partner.

Step 3. Do you think Gordon knows how to run the press? Do you think Ali should follow Gordon's instructions? If not, what should Ali do now? Discuss this question with your partner.

Step 4. Continue the conversation. Student A: Take Ali's part and tell Gordon what you're going to do. You are very safety conscious. Student B: Take Gordon's part. You usually come up with your own way of doing things rather than following procedures. Change roles.

6 Read and Write

Step 1. Read the memo below from a safety inspector. Find out where the company had safety problems.

The following items were safety violations noted upon inspection of company premises on November 21, 1996. All violations must be corrected within 5 working days.
1) Front lobby area: electrical cords with exposed, frayed wires
2) Office: supply boxes blocking air ventilation
3) Dining room: serving carts in heavy traffic areas; inadequate lighting at exits
4) Kitchen: food boxes on floors; no safety signage; appliance wires near faucets

Step 2. Complete this safety checklist with the information from the memo. Put a check mark (✔) for areas that passed inspection (that is, no violation was mentioned in the memo). Put an asterisk (*) for areas where there were problems.

	Lighting	Walkways	Wiring	Storage	Safety Signage
Front lobby					
Office					
Dining room					
Kitchen					

Step 3. This time, imagine you are the safety inspector who filled out the checklist below. The boxes with a ✔ indicate areas that passed inspection. Those with an * did not pass for the reasons listed below the chart. Read the chart to find out which departments had safety problems.

	Wiring	Storage	Equipment	Walkways
Reception	*	✔	✔	✔
Accounting	✔	*	✔	✔
Human Resources	✔	✔	✔	✔
Assembly	*	*	*	*
Shipping	✔	✔	✔	*

Notes:
1) Recep: phone wires extending from north wall to desk on west wall
2) Acctg: heavy boxes stacked on top of file cabinets
3) Asmbl: total lack of organization; several electrical cords crossing on floors between machinery; several tool boxes extending out from under work tables; equipment blocking walkways at two locations; unidentified liquid spilled on floor near electrical source
4) Shpng: exit blocked by boxes of supplies

Step 4. Inform the company of the areas where they did not pass inspection. Write a memo like the one in Step 1 listing all of the safety problems you found.

Step 5. With a partner, compare your work. Discuss any necessary corrections.

Form and Function

1 Why don't we tell Rita about this?

Why don't we tell Rita about this?   =   Let's tell Rita about this.
We should tell Rita about this.

(Requests for information)   *(Answers)*
A: Why don't we turn in our timesheets   B: Because the company changed
   on Friday?   the system.
A: Why isn't this working?   B: Because someone dropped it.

Examples

A: The photocopier isn't working. There's a paper jam.
B: Oh, **why don't** you open the photocopier and take a look inside?

A: We don't have enough money in the budget for everything we need.
B: Well, then, **why don't** we have a meeting and talk about possible solutions?
A: That's a good idea.

Practice 1

A. Listen and decide if you are hearing a request for information or a problem-solving suggestion.

1. ____ request for information   ✔ problem-solving suggestion

2. ____ request for information   ____ problem-solving suggestion

3. ____ request for information   ____ problem-solving suggestion

4. ____ request for information   ____ problem-solving suggestion

5. ____ request for information   ____ problem-solving suggestion

B. With a partner, write two short conversations. In the first one, write a request for information. In the second, write a problem-solving suggestion as a solution to a simple problem. For the request for information, many forms are possible.

Example:

Request for information: A: Why doesn't the fax machine work?
                                  B: Someone turned it off.

Problem-solving suggestion: A: There's a large grease spill on the floor.
                                  B: Yes, there is. Why don't we get some rags and clean it up?

C. Work with a partner. Choose two of the safety problems below and role-play a short conversation for each. Make a suggestion to solve each problem.

- Dangerous chemicals are leaking from a vat.
- There is a pile of papers next to a heat source.
- A typewriter has a frayed wire.
- Boxes are blocking an emergency exit.

2 We had finished the project by the time he arrived to help us.

Emphasis: *Before* and *After*

| I, you, he, she, it, we, they | **had** | finish**ed** | the project <u>by the time</u> he **arrived**. |
| | **hadn't** | | |

Emphasis: Sequence of Events

We **finished** the project, and then he **arrived**.
I **went** out, **came** back at 2:00, and then **started** to work again.

Examples

We **had seen** him around town many times before we met him.
Susan and Nick **had worked** here ten years before I came.
Had anyone **gone** in that room before Jack locked it?

Practice 2

A. Listen. Put a (1) next to the action that occurred first, and a (2) next to the action that occurred second.

1. __2__ Sylvia left for work.

   __1__ I called her.

2. _____ The firemen arrived.

   _____ We put the fire out.

3. _____ They didn't speak to each other.

   _____ They saw each other.

4. _____ My boss left.

   _____ I finished my work.

5. _____ I didn't live in California.

   _____ I moved here.

6. _____ We worked independently.

   _____ They put us on teams.

B. Complete the sentences using the verbs and any other words in parentheses. Use the correct forms of the verbs.

1. I (eat) _____ *had eaten* _____ dinner already by the time my husband (get)

   _____ home last night.

2. JoAnn was really nervous about meeting with her supervisor yesterday. He (just) (fire)

   _____ three people before JoAnn (see) _____ him.

3. Dave is glad his boss (return) _____ last Monday. He (not) (write down)

   _____ any instructions for Dave before he (leave) _____.

C. Look at Barbara's schedule for yesterday. What did she do? When? Write three sentences about her.

Example:

The newspaper had arrived when Barbara got up.

5:30	newspaper arrived	8:30	talked to boss
6:30	got up	9:30	started new project
7:30	got to work	11:30	had lunch with Rosemary

D. Work with a partner. Student A: Look at this page. Student B: Look at page 84. The chart below shows what several people did last year and when. Some of the information is missing. Ask questions and complete the chart. Use the correct forms of the verbs.

Example:

A: When did **Victoria move**?
B: **She moved in June**.
A: Had **she** already **gotten engaged** when **she moved**?
B: **No, she didn't get engaged until September.**

Person	Action 1	Month	Action 2	Month
Tony	buy a new car		get a raise	
Victoria	move	June	get engaged	September
Al	quit his job		get a new job	
Rhoda	get a promotion	April	change shifts	March

Work with a partner. Student B: Look at this page. Student A: Look at page 83. The chart below shows what several people did last year and when. Some of the information is missing. Ask questions and complete the chart. Use the correct forms of the verbs.

Example:
A: When did **Tony buy a new car**?
B: **He bought it in February**.
A: Had **he** already **gotten a raise** when **he bought it**?
B: **No, he didn't get a raise until May.**

Person	Action 1	Month	Action 2	Month
Tony	buy a new car	February	get a raise	May
Victoria	move		get engaged	
Al	quit his job	March	get a new job	May
Rhoda	get a promotion		change shifts	

E. Now write sentences about all of the people in the chart.

1. (Tony) _____

2. (Victoria) _____

3. (Al) _____

4. (Rhoda) _____

F. What about you? Think about what you did last year. What were some significant events? When did they happen? Were they happy occasions? How did they make you feel?

Student A: Tell your partner about the three most important things that happened to you last year. Were you glad they happened? Did you make them happen or did they happen to you?

Student B: Ask your partner for details about the events. How did he/she feel about them at the time? How does he/she feel about them now?

Add your own questions and then change roles.

1 Pair Work

Step 1. Listen. With a partner, complete the instructions for using a fire extinguisher.

_____ handles _____ ringpin

_____ nozzle at base of _____

_____ upright _____ side to side _____

_____ back six feet from _____

Step 2. Arrange the instructions in order from the first thing you should do to the last. Check with another pair of students. Do you agree?

Step 3. Why is it important to follow the instructions in the correct order? What might happen if someone tried to use this equipment without knowing the proper procedures? What can you do to prevent a problem like this from occurring at your workplace? Discuss this with your partner and another pair of students.

2 Pair Work

Step 1. Role-play.

Student A: You are a supervisor and you have a new employee in your department. You need to teach him/her some basic safety rules (including how to use a fire extinguisher), but he/she doesn't understand English very well. You don't speak his/her native language. You are a little bit frustrated, and you ask another supervisor for help.

Student B: You are another supervisor at this company. Give Student A some suggestions for ways to teach basic safety to his/her new employee. Think about your experience learning English as a second language and methods that helped you understand instructions in a new language.

Step 2. With your partner, make a list of the methods Student B suggested for teaching basic safety to a new employee. With another pair of students, compare your list.

3 Group/Class Work

Step 1. In a group, choose any kind of workplace (factory, restaurant, office, store). Work together to brainstorm safety issues that would be particularly important for that kind of workplace. Think about different kinds of potential safety problems, including the following:

1. working with tools, equipment, and/or chemicals or other products
2. work space and environment
3. personal safety outside premises (location of worksite, graveyard shifts, etc.)
4. public access to work areas

Step 2. Identify your group's five most important safety issues. Now brainstorm ways to address each of those issues in the workplace to prevent potential problems from happening.

Step 3. Elect a spokesperson to present your group's issues and solutions to the class. Be prepared to answer questions from the class.

4 Culture Work

Safety issues are a serious concern of many employers in the United States. Many employers are even more concerned about safety when their employees' native languages are other than English. Some employers feel that such employees might endanger themselves and their co-workers on the job.

Why do you think some employers feel this way? How could your ability to speak English affect your safety on the job? How could it affect others' safety? Discuss this with the class.

Think about the safety issues and solutions you discussed earlier in your groups. Would any issues or solutions need to be changed in any way if a large number of employees were not native English speakers? If so, how could they be changed to include such employees?

Return to your groups and imagine that at least half of your workforce speaks English as a second language with varying ability. Discuss any modifications you might need to make to your list of issues and solutions. Then present your group's ideas to the class with reasons for making changes or not making changes.

Are there immigrant workers in your native country? If so, what are some of the issues that concern employers about hiring them? How do you feel about employers in your native country who hire or refuse to hire immigrants? Discuss this with the class.

Unit 8
OPERATING INSTRUCTIONS

Openers

Look at the picture. Find the pieces of equipment below.

a fax   a computer   a copier   a printer

We have many kinds of equipment at work and at home to help us do our work.
Where are these pieces of equipment often found? Have you used any of the equipment
in the picture?

1 Listen and Think

Listen. Then answer the questions with a partner.

1. Why did Rita stop Ali?

2. What is Rita having a problem with?

3. Is Ali able to help Rita with her problem?

4. What does Ali suggest Rita do to get help?

5. Can you think of anything else Rita could do?

2 Talk to a Partner

Step 1. Practice the conversation with a partner.

A: Hi, Janet. Do you have a minute?

J: Sure. What can I do for you?

A: Well, I was trying to send a fax when the machine
just went off. Ali said you might know something
about it since you used to work over here.

J: Haven't you ever learned how to use it?

A: Yes, I did when I was new. I had been working
here for a long time, and then they transferred me to shipping
last year, so I haven't used it for over a year now.

J: Oh, well, I can go over it with you right now if you want.
In fact, why don't you get out the operating manual, and we'll
take a look at it.

A: OK, thanks. I really appreciate your help.

**Step 2. Choose a piece of equipment you know about, or choose one from the picture
dictionary in the back of the book. Role-play a similar conversation.**

3 Read and Think

Step 1. Read the text below.

After Janet helped Rita get started, Rita found the operating manual for her fax machine. Like most
operating instructions, the first part showed a diagram of the machine with the names of all of the
main parts, controls, and levers.

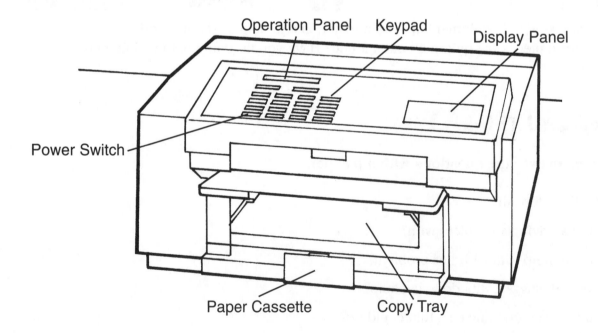

Step 2. Read the text.

Sometimes there is not enough space on the diagram to show the names of the parts, so a letter or number is substituted for each named part. The names of the parts are then listed with their corresponding letters or numbers near the diagram.

Vocabulary

controls knobs and dials that can be adjusted to change various aspects of a machine's operation

corresponding belonging to; matching

diagram a drawing or photograph with information added

lever a type of control shaped like a handle; the handle is moved into one of only two or three positions such as "on/off" or "high/medium/low" to adjust a machine's operation

substituted put in place of

Step 3. Read the text below.

Besides diagrams, operating instructions also include information on how to use the machine (basic operation), what to do if something goes wrong (often called "troubleshooting"), and safety information.

Step 4. Read the following instructions. With a partner, decide if they are providing information on (1) basic operation, (2) troubleshooting, or (3) safety. Write the number (1, 2, or 3) corresponding to the type of instruction next to each sentence.

_1_	Press the power knob to start the machine.
_____	Keep the electrical cords away from heat and water sources.
_____	If the power signal light flashes, turn the machine off and check the electrical cords to be sure they are properly connected.
_____	While the machine is running, adjust speed control as necessary.
_____	Do not touch any parts colored orange while the machine is on. These parts become extremely hot during operation.
_____	If beep sounds when pressing the start button, refer to the display panel for the location of the problem.

Vocabulary

as necessary if and when you think you need to

display panel a window showing information to the person using the machine; information might be shown with lights, numbers, or abbreviated words

flash go on and off repeatedly and quickly

signal an indication of some kind, usually a light or a sound

Complete the sentences with the correct words.

display panel   signal   substitute   flashing

1. Why don't we _____*substitute*_____ the red wires for the green ones since we don't have any green ones?

2. Sue kept hearing a beep on her computer, but she didn't understand what that

   _____ meant.

3. A: Why is that red light _____ on the copier?
   B: It means we need to change the toner.

4. A: How can you tell when the copier is out of paper?

   B: The little paper symbol will show up on the _____.

4 Put It in Writing

Step 1. Think of a machine you know how to operate either from your workplace or at home. Write three sentences giving basic operation information.

Example: *Turn the volume control knob to adjust the volume as necessary.*

1. _____

2. _____

3. _____

Step 2. Now write three sentences that give troubleshooting information for the same machine.

Example: *If the copies appear too light, check the toner.*

1. _____

2. _____

3. _____

Step 1. Rita has almost finished the project she's working on, but there's a problem with the machine. Listen to Rita's conversation with John.

A: I've got a problem here that I can't figure out.

B: What's going on?

A: Well, you see that "ERROR" message on the display panel? The machine won't run until I correct that.

B: It says "Error–A-3." What does the message mean?

A: "A-3" is supposed to be the location of the problem, but I can't tell what's wrong. The machine had been running great all day, but at five to five it suddenly just stopped.

Step 2. Practice the conversation with a partner.

Step 3. Continue the conversation. Student A: Suggest something Rita might do to resolve the problem. Student B: What do you think of your partner's suggestion? Have you already tried it? Have you already considered it? Change roles and add a different ending to the conversation.

Here are some possible suggestions for Rita. Add your own.

Rita might be able to get someone from the maintenance department to help.
Rita might need to call the supervisor for help.

_____   _____

_____   _____

Step 4. With another pair of classmates, compare the suggestions you made. Which ones do you think are reasonable? Which ones would you follow in Rita's place?

6 Read and Write

Step 1. Imagine that you work in a hotel and you must complete the inventory control sheet below for all of the equipment in the hotel. In order to do this, you must look at each piece of equipment on page 122 in the back of the book and copy the serial number onto the form.

SLEEPYTIME HOTEL
Inventory Control

Name: _____ Date: _____

_____

DEPARTMENT	EQUIPMENT	SERIAL NUMBER
FRONT DESK	computer	
	fax	
	printer	
KITCHEN	oven	
	grill	
	refrigerator	
LAUNDRY	washer	
	dryer	
HOUSEKEEPING/MAINTENANCE	vacuum cleaner	
	floor buffer	
	power drill	

Step 2. With a partner, compare your answers.

Form and Function

1 I was trying to send a fax when the machine just stopped working.

<table>
<tr><td></td><td>——————→</td><td></td><td></td><td></td><td>X</td></tr>
<tr><td>I, he, she, (it) was
wasn't
we, you, they were
weren't</td><td>trying</td><td>to . . .</td><td><u>when</u> the machine</td><td></td><td>stopped.</td></tr>
<tr><td>Was I, he, she, (it)
Were we, you, they</td><td>trying</td><td>to . . .</td><td><u>when</u> the machine</td><td></td><td>stopped?</td></tr>
<tr><td>What was I, he, she, (it)
were we, you, they</td><td>trying</td><td>to (do)</td><td><u>when</u> the machine</td><td></td><td>stopped?</td></tr>
</table>

Examples

I **was typing** a document on my computer <u>when</u> the screen **went** blank.
<u>When</u> she **called**, I **was sending** a fax.
A: **What were** you **doing** <u>when</u> the problem **occurred**? B: I **was dialing** a number.

Practice 1

A. Listen to the sentences. For each sentence, decide if the verb below is for the shorter action or the longer action.

1. do   shorter   (longer)   4. fix   shorter   longer

2. work   shorter   longer   5. tell   shorter   longer

3. turn   shorter   longer   6. start shorter   longer

B. Look at the pictures below. On a separate sheet of paper, write a sentence for each picture. Then, with a partner, compare your sentences.

C. With a partner, tell a story about a problem you have had with a piece of equipment or machinery of any kind. Describe what happened and what you were doing when the problem occurred. Did you solve the problem yourself, or did you have to report it to someone? Tell your partner.

Example: Once I was working on a punch press, and I pressed the wrong button, and the machine jammed. I couldn't figure out how to fix it, so I reported the problem to my supervisor.

2 This machine had been running fine for hours when it suddenly just stopped.

I, you, he, she, it, we, they	**had been working**	when it stopped.
I, you, he, she, it, we, they	**had not been working**	long when it stopped.
Had it	**been working**	long when it stopped?

Examples

I **had been working** there a year when the company went out of business.
Mary and Carl **had been dating** for six months when they broke up.
A: **How long had** the light **been flashing** when you turned the machine off?
B: I guess it **had been flashing** for about five minutes.

Practice 2

A. Listen. Circle the correct answer.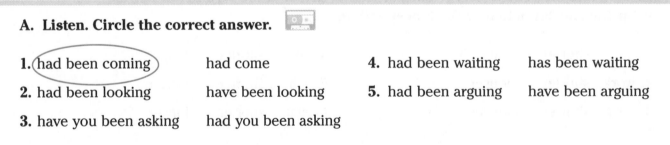

1. ⟨had been coming⟩   had come   **4.** had been waiting   has been waiting

2. had been looking   have been looking   **5.** had been arguing   have been arguing

3. have you been asking   had you been asking

B. Fill in the blanks with the correct forms of the verbs in parentheses. Add any additional words you need to put the verbs in their correct forms.

1. Mark (work) _had been working_ in the shipping office for three years when he finally (get)

got a promotion.

2. Rene and Flora (play) _____ tennis for about six months when they (win)

_____ that tournament.

3. A: I (find) _____ a job!

   B: Oh. I didn't know you (look) _____ for one.

4. A: We should send Bob Thomas a sympathy card. His father (die) _____.

   B: (be) (he) _____ ill very long?

5. I don't know why Ann was so mad. She (wait) _____ only a half hour or

so when I (pick up) (her) _____.

C. Work with a partner. Student A: Look at this page. Student B: Look at page 96.

Imagine your company has begun to document equipment failures. The company wants to know how long it takes employees to report problems in order to speed up repairs. The chart below shows when several people reported problems with their equipment last month. Ask questions and complete the chart. Use the correct forms of the verbs.

Example:

B: How long **had Mike's computer been overheating** when **he** reported it?
A: It had been **overheating** for **two days**.
B: When did **he** report the problem?
A: **He** reported it on **January 8th.**

Person	Date of Report	Type of Problem	Duration of Problem
Mike	1-8	computer overheating	2 days
Sarah		power light flashing	
Frank	1-11	forklift not lifting	8 hours
Pete		copier paper jamming	
Carmen	1-4	phones not working	10 minutes
Greg		press levers lowering too fast	

Work with a partner. Student B: Look at this page. Student A: Look at page 95.

Imagine your company has begun to document equipment failures. The company wants to know how long it takes employees to report problems in order to speed up repairs. The chart below shows when several people reported problems with their equipment last month. Ask questions and complete the chart. Use the correct forms of the verbs.

Example:

A: How long **had Sarah's power light been flashing** when **she** reported it?
B: It had been **flashing** for **four days**.
A: When did **she** report the problem?
B: **She** reported it on **January 22nd**.

Person	Date of Report	Type of problem	Duration of problem
Mike		computer overheating	
Sarah	1-22	power light flashing	4 days
Frank		forklift not lifting	
Pete	1-14	copier paper jamming	2 hours
Carmen		phones not working	
Greg	1-29	press levers lowering too fast	2 weeks

D. Now write sentences about all of the people and their equipment.

1. (Mike) _____

2. (Sarah) _____

3. (Frank) _____

4. (Pete) _____

5. (Carmen) _____

6. (Greg) _____

Putting It to Work

1 Pair Work

Step 1. Listen. With a partner, fill in the missing information from the operating instructions below for a paper shredder.

---

1. Before _____ the power on, check all electrical cords.

2. To increase the speed, slowly turn the _____ knob to the right (clockwise).

3. To turn the power off, lower the power _____ to the "off" position.

4. If the red light flashes during _____, turn the power off immediately.

5. If the error _____ (yellow light) appears, consult the operations manual for further instructions.

6. Avoid _____ this equipment for more than twelve hours a day.

7. Always wear protective gloves when _____ this equipment.

Step 2. Role-play a conversation between a new employee and an employee who knows this piece of equipment well. Explain to the new employee how to use the equipment. Choose the most important points. Change roles.

2 Pair Work

Step 1. Role-play. Imagine you and your partner work the same position on different shifts.

Student A: At the end of your shift, you are having trouble with the equipment you work on. You had been trying to fix the problem for a while when your co-worker arrived to relieve you. You must explain as much as you know about the problem and what you had been doing to try to fix it.

Student B: You arrive to start your shift and discover your equipment is down. You need to find out as much as you can from your co-worker on the previous shift before he/she leaves.

Step 2. Since this is not the first time this problem has occurred, you and your partner decide the problem must be reported to your supervisor, but he/she has already gone home. Work together to write a memo to your supervisor about the problem, what you did about it, and whether or not you have resolved it.

3 Group/Class Work

Step 1. In a group, choose a piece of equipment or some kind of machine that you all know. It can be something in your classroom, something you use at home, or something from work.

Step 2. Work together to plan and design an operating instructions manual for your equipment. Be sure to include diagrams, basic operating instructions, troubleshooting advice, and safety information. Think about ways to make the manual easier to use (more "user-friendly") for people with no experience using this equipment. How can you make it more user-friendly for people whose first language is not English?

Step 3. Develop your operations manual and prepare to present it to the rest of the class. Choose someone from your group to be the trainer.

Step 4. Ask for a volunteer from the class to be the trainee. The trainer will train the trainee on the equipment, using the manual as a reference as necessary. The trainee should ask lots of questions.

Step 5. Ask the class to critique your manual. Was it useful for training? Did it answer the questions the trainee asked? Was it well organized and user-friendly? How might your group be able to improve the manual?

4 Culture Work

With the class, discuss the following questions:

1. In your native country, what happens when machinery or equipment breaks down?

2. When you have problems with a piece of equipment, do you report it to someone who can fix it?

3. What responsibility do employees have to keep equipment in good condition?

4. What responsibility does company management have to provide equipment that is safe and in good working order?

5. In what situations or jobs does equipment belong specifically to employees, and what is their responsibility for this equipment?

6. Does work become easier when companies buy more and better equipment? Give examples of situations you know.

7. In your work situation, what kinds of suggestions would you make about the use and maintenance of equipment if you could make suggestions anonymously (without giving your name)?

8. What kinds of suggestions would you make openly?

Unit 9
REPORTING EMERGENCIES

Openers

Look at the pictures. Match each one to one of these words.

flood   fire   explosion   earthquake

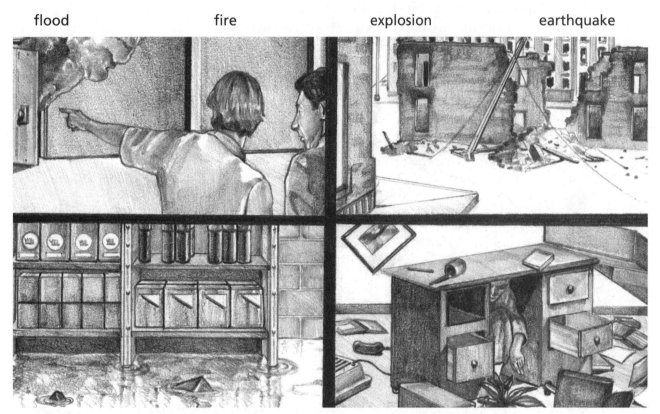

What is happening in the pictures? Has anything like this ever happened to you or anyone you know? What would you do if an emergency like one of the ones above happened at your workplace?

1 Listen and Think

Listen. Then answer the questions with a partner.

1. What did the first man ask the other at the beginning of the conversation?

2. What is happening at their workplace?

3. How does each man react?

4. Which reaction do you think is better? Why?

5. Why do you think the first man wants to know what's in the storeroom?

6. Why doesn't the other man want to open the storeroom door?

2 Talk to a Partner

Step 1. Practice the conversation with a partner.

A: Hi, this is Chuck.
B: Chuck, this is Yolanda. I'm on the second floor, and it looks like there's a fire in the storeroom.
A: Is anybody hurt?
B: No, we're all fine. There's smoke coming out from the storeroom, but the door's closed so I'm not sure how bad it is. Eric went to pull the fire alarm.
A: Good. I'll call the fire department. Make sure everyone gets out of there right away, and I'll meet you all down here.
B: OK. We'll be down in a minute. Hopefully, if they get here in time, there won't be a lot of damage.

Step 2. With your partner, look at the pictures below. For each picture, name the emergency and discuss who you would call to report the emergency.

Step 3. Role-play. With your partner, choose two of the situations and practice reporting each emergency.

3 Read and Think

Step 1.   Read the text below.

In any emergency situation, whether it happens at home or at work, the first priority is to help and protect people. This includes you, anyone else at the scene, and anyone who might arrive at the scene of the emergency. This also means that putting yourself in danger to help someone else might end up putting both of you in even more danger. Whenever possible, it is best to wait for professionals such as police and fire departments to arrive.

Because events happen so quickly in an emergency, it is often difficult to describe exactly what happened. If you find yourself in an emergency, try to be as aware as you can of what is going on around you. When you report the emergency, you will be asked many questions and you will be asked to describe what happened. It is very important to stay as calm as you possibly can; you will be able to get better assistance if you can calmly and accurately describe the situation for the people you call for help.

Vocabulary

aware conscious and alert

calm not nervous; relaxed

describe tell someone about something so that he or she can picture it

emergency a sudden, unexpected occurrence demanding immediate action

events occurrences; things that happen

scene the place where something happens

Step 2.   Read the following brief descriptions and match each one to one of the emergency situations on page 99.

- When I got out of my car in the parking lot, I heard a loud noise, and everything shook for a second. I saw smoke in the distance. _____

- Everything just started shaking. It must have gone on for a couple of minutes I looked around, and everything was moving—the lights, the pictures, everything. _____

- When I arrived at the building, I saw Alicia outside on the ground. She was in a lot of pain. Flames were coming from the building. _____

- I don't know where all that water came from—maybe a pipe broke or something. The water must have been four or five inches deep already when I got there.

  _____

Step 3. **Read the following excerpt from a manual on emergency procedures.**

In Case of Emergency

Knowing what to do in case of an emergency can often save time and unnecessary anxiety when an emergency actually occurs. Your employer should provide you with some training in handling emergencies. For example, there should be information at your workplace about what to do in case of a fire. The information should include a map of the workplace showing exit routes from all work stations. Your employer may even conduct drills from time to time so that you and your co-workers can actually practice what to do and where to go. If you don't have any or all of this information about your workplace, ask for it now. Don't wait for an emergency to find out.

911

The 24-hour emergency assistance telephone number throughout the United States is 911. Dialing that number puts you in touch with a dispatcher. Once you describe the emergency to the dispatcher, he/she will decide what type of assistance you need and send someone to help you. Many people panic in an emergency and speak very quickly or begin to cry while they are speaking. You must remember to speak slowly and clearly so the dispatcher can understand you.

Vocabulary

anxiety nervousness
assistance help
dispatcher a person at a central location who coordinates services to certain areas or locations

drills practices that simulate an actual event such as an emergency
in case of in the event of; if something happens
panic get too nervous about a situation; become terrified

Practice

Complete the sentences with the correct words or phrases.

assistance	in case of	panic	calm	describe

1. When you call 911, you have to _____*describe*_____ what happened so they can help you.

2. _____ a fire, pull the fire alarm and leave the building as quickly as possible.

3. It's important to stay _____ during an emergency so that you can help people and follow instructions.

4. If people are hurt during an emergency, it's usually better to wait for professional

_____ instead of trying to help them yourself.

5. Whatever you do, don't _____; you won't be able to help anyone or yourself if you are crying or screaming.

4 Put It in Writing

Step 1. Think of an accident or emergency that you were involved in or that you witnessed. It can be something that happened at work or somewhere else, and it does not need to be a major event (for example, when you cut your finger or when your child fell). Make notes on a separate sheet of paper about that event.

Step 2. Write three or four sentences describing what happened. Be sure to include where it happened, any people besides yourself who were involved, and any damages or injuries that resulted.

Example:

When I got out of my car one night, I hit my head on one of the boxes in the garage. I had a small cut on my forehead over my right eye, but I didn't need to see a doctor for it.

_____

_____

_____

_____

Step 3. With a partner, tell each other about your accidents or emergencies.

Step 4. Now write three or four sentences about your partner's accident or emergency based on what he/she told you. Ask any questions you need to in order to report on the event.

_____

_____

_____

_____

5 Listen and Speak

Step 1. Lena witnessed an accident at work and is telling her supervisor what happened. But Lena hesitates to describe everything. Listen to the conversation.

Supervisor: Thanks for coming in, Lena. Tell me what you saw.

Lena: Well, it all happened so fast, I'm not sure. But I think John was just working on that press and it came down on his hand.

Supervisor: Was anyone else there when it happened?

Lena: Well, uh, yeah. Well, John was talking to someone.

Supervisor: Do you know who it was?

Lena: I think it's one of the maintenance guys. I've seen him around, but I know he doesn't work in our department. If you asked someone else, you would probably get a better idea of the situation.

Supervisor: OK, Lena. Well, thanks for the information.

Step 2. Practice the conversation with a partner.

Step 3. What do you think will happen next? Student A: Imagine you are the supervisor and continue your investigation of the accident. Student B: Play the role of whoever the supervisor calls next. Have a conversation about the accident.

After this second conversation, does the supervisor have a complete description of the accident? Why or why not? What do you think the supervisor will have to do next?

Step 4. Role-play your conversation for another pair of students and then listen to their conversation. Compare the situations. Are they similar?

6 Read and Write

Step 1. Read the information in Read and Think on pages 101–102 again. Based on this information and your own knowledge of emergency procedures, write a list of things to do and not to do when responding to emergencies.

DO	DON'T

Step 2. Compare your list with a partner. Combine your lists to make a more complete list.

Form and Function

1 Hopefully, if they get here in time, there won't be a lot of damage.

If they	**get**	here in time,	**there will not (won't) be** a lot of damage.
	don't get		**there will be**
If	**Juan doesn't get**	a new job,	**he won't earn** more money.
If	**he gets**	a new job,	**will he earn** more money?

Examples

If I get a job in California, **I'll move** in with my brother.
If you ask Mr. Jones for a raise, **will he give** it to you?
If JoAnn doesn't get that promotion, **she'll quit** next week.

Practice 1

A. Listen. Circle all the things Carlos says he will do if he becomes president of the employees' association.

1. (He'll work hard.)

2. He'll get a raise.

3. He'll ask for better benefits.

4. He'll make changes.

5. He'll be sorry.

B. Now write three sentences about Carlos's promises.

Example: *If Carlos becomes president, he'll work hard.*

1. _____

2. _____

3. _____

C. Fill in the blanks with the correct forms of the verbs in parentheses. Use any other words in parentheses correctly in combination with the verbs.

1. If Tom (come) ___*comes*___ to work late again today, his supervisor (give)

   ___*will give*___ him a warning.

2. If they (not) (train) _____ the new employees, they (not) (know)

   _____ how to use any of this equipment.

3. If Sarah and Jim (get) (marry) _____, (they) (have to) _____
   move?

4. If I (not) (see) _____ you after the meeting, I (call) _____
   you tonight.

5. If we (not) (finish) _____ this work order today, we (not) (be able to) (ship)

   _____ it out tomorrow.

D. Imagine that you work for a company that has announced it will have to lay off 10 percent of the workforce. What will you do if you are laid off? Will you look for another job? If so, how will you look? On a separate sheet of paper, write five sentences about what you will do. Then tell a classmate.

2 If you asked someone else, you would get a better idea of the situation.

If	you **asked** someone else,	you **would get** a better idea.
If	I **had** more time,	I **would go** back to college.
If	I **didn't have** so much work,	I **would go** back to college.
If	you **had** more time,	**would** you **go** back to college?

Examples

If they **had** more money, they **wouldn't fight** so much.
If they **didn't have** so many children, they **would go** out to eat more often.
If this company **gave** us better health insurance, we **would** all **be** much happier.

Practice 2

A. Listen to the speakers tell what they would do if they won the lottery. Circle the correct answer for each statement.

1. (quit job)   keep working

2. give some money to charity   keep all the money

3. buy a new house   buy my parents a new house

4. take a trip to Hawaii   move to Hawaii

5. put some money in the bank   put all the money in the bank

B. Fill in the blanks with the correct forms of the verbs in parentheses. Use any other words in parentheses correctly in combination with the verbs.

1. If I (earn) _____*earned*_____ more money here, I (not) (have to get)

   __*wouldn't have to get*__ a second job.

2. If we (live) _____ in the suburbs, we (spend) _____ three
   hours a day driving back and forth to work.

3. If you (be) _____ our supervisor, (you) (make) _____ us fill
   out these reports every day?

4. If Jane (be) (not) _____ married, I (ask) _____ her out.

5. If you (have) _____ a million dollars, (what) (you) (do)

   _____?

C. Work with a partner. Student A: Look at this page. Student B: Look at page 108. The chart below shows what several people would do if they were in a management position at the company they work for. Some of the information is missing. Ask questions and complete the chart. Use the correct forms of the verbs.

Example:

B: What would **John** do if **he became the owner of the company?**

A: If **John became the owner of the company, he'd expand the company.**

Person/Change in Position	Action
John—owner of the company	expand the company
Claire—supervisor	
Fred—president	improve everyone's benefits
Amy—head of security	

Work with a partner. Student B: Look at this page. Student A: Look at page 107. The chart below shows what several people would do if they were in a management position at the company they work for. Some of the information is missing. Ask questions and complete the chart. Use the correct forms of the verbs.

Example:

A: What would **Claire** do if **she became supervisor?**

B: If **Claire became supervisor, she'd eliminate overtime.**

Person/Change in Position	Action
John—owner of the company	
Claire—supervisor	eliminate overtime
Fred—president	
Amy—head of security	hire at least ten more guards

D. Now write sentences about all the people in the chart.

1. (John) _____

2. (Claire) _____

3. (Fred) _____

4. (Amy) _____

E. Discussion.

How would you improve things at your workplace if you were in a different position? What would you improve? What position would you have to hold in order to do what you would like to do?

Tell a partner. Then listen to his/her ideas. Ask each other questions about the current situations at your workplaces and why you would like to improve them.

Putting It to Work

1 Pair Work

Step 1. Listen to each description or report. With a partner, decide what each problem is from the list. Make notes about each problem.

robbery   earthquake   fire   accident   power outage

	Problem	Notes
1.		
2.		
3.		
4.		
5.		

Step 2. Role-play. Choose one of the problems above. Imagine that you and your partner were in that situation.

Student A: Imagine you are reporting the emergency. You are extremely nervous and upset. You are new to this country, and sometimes you can't think of the words you need to say. This makes you even more upset. Tell your partner as well as you can what happened, what the current situation is, and whether anybody is hurt. Answer any questions he/she asks you.

Student B: Imagine you are taking the report. You need to get as much information as you can in order to decide what to do. You are having some trouble understanding the person who is reporting to you, and you need to ask several questions to get better information.

Step 3. With your partner, write a brief report of the emergency based on the information you exchanged in Step 2. Be sure to consider which information is the most important. Include as many details as possible. Is your report complete? If not, what other information would you need if you were actually reporting such an emergency?

Step 4. With your partner, write a list of the questions that your report does not answer. Compare your list of questions with another pair of classmates. Do you have similar questions on your lists? Which questions do you think would be the most important to answer if you were ever actually in such an emergency?

2 Group/Class Work

Step 1. In a group, consider the location where your class takes place. Work together to develop emergency procedures for the area. Be sure to include procedures for all kinds of emergencies. Think about how to handle any injured people, how to get more assistance, and how to report emergencies that might occur. What training, if any, would your classmates need in order to follow these procedures? What equipment and/or supplies are needed in order to be prepared for an emergency?

Step 2. Put together an emergency procedures manual for the classroom. You might want to include written materials, diagrams or drawings, and/or lists of things to remember in case of emergency.

Step 3. Present your manual to the rest of the class. Tell them the reasons your group decided to include the information that appears in the manual. Be prepared to answer any questions the rest of the class might ask you.

3 Culture Work

Step 1. With the class, discuss the following questions:

1. What are the ways that people help each other in emergencies?

2. What kinds of planning and preparation do you do in your city or town to handle emergencies?

3. How do people handle emergencies in your native country?

4. How do the local authorities deal with an emergency in your city or town? in your native country?

Step 2. Divide into groups. Write a group letter about emergency procedures in the United States. Write to someone who is not from this country. Write about the aspects of safety and emergency preparation you find unusual in the United States, and explain everything your reader needs to know.

Step 3. A member of your group will read your letter to the class.

Unit 10
COMPANY HEALTH PLANS

Openers

Look at the picture. How do the words below apply to the situation you see?

patient   health care   insurance   employees

Where is Rita? What is happening? Have you or anyone you know ever had a similar experience in this country?

1 Listen and Think

Listen and answer T for True or F for False.

1. The new plan has more than one choice.   (T)   F

2. Almost all employees will pay less in health-care premiums if they choose the HMO.   T   F

3. The company is introducing the HMO even though it will cost more.   T   F

4. Employees can change plans every six months.   T   F

2 Talk to a Partner

Step 1. With a partner, practice the conversation.

A: So, let's begin. What are your questions?

B: An obvious question: how much is deducted from our paychecks now?

A: That depends on the plan. If you take the HMO, it's less. All of the figures are shown on the information sheet in your packet.

B: OK. Now I pay a deductible of $600 a year for my family. What about the new plan?

A: OK, the deductible depends on the coverage you choose.

B: How much choice of doctors and hospitals is there? I hope my doctor is on the new list.

A: Well, the list is in your packet. You can check there to see if your doctor is on it.

Step 2. With a partner, think of other questions that you would want to ask about the plans.

3 Read and Think

Step 1. Below is the company memo that announced the meeting (above). Read it and underline the two reasons why the company likes the new health plan. Then answer the questions that follow.

TO: All Full-Time Employees
FROM: Mary
RE: Health Insurance
DATE: October 3, 1996

On Thursday, October 10, 1996, we will be holding a meeting to discuss a new health insurance plan for our employees and their families. If you are interested in joining or continuing your health insurance with the company plan, please plan to attend.

The rates are better than what we have been paying for our old plan, and we feel the choices are better, too. Each participating employee will now have the choice of three different plans. You may choose the plan that best suits your needs.

If you have questions prior to the meeting or wish to review the booklets about these plans, please contact Connie or Mary in the main office.

---

1. Do all employees participate in the company health plan?
2. Do workers in your country have more than one option for health insurance?

Vocabulary

booklet little book or informational brochure

deductible in insurance, the part of the costs you have to pay first before the insurance pays the rest of the costs

memo (or memorandum) an official notice which is distributed internally in a company

plan an organized arrangement

prior to before, in advance of (something)

Step 2. The document below was given out at the health-care plan meeting at Seton Foods on October 10th. Compare these health insurance rates.

CURRENT RATES (Old HMO Plan)

Single coverage   Family coverage
$ 114.70 per month $ 298.06 per month

The attached list shows the rates for the new plans. The figures shown are what it costs each employee per month for the various plans. (Seton Foods continues to pay 50% of the total premium cost.)

TRUE CARE HEALTH SERVICES QUALITY HEALTH OPTIONS PLANS

Your rates under TRUE CARE's group of plans are as follows:

	TRUE CARE Staff HMO Plan	IPA HMO Plan	PPO Plan
Employee rate	$ 69.96/mo.	$ 78.54/mo.	$ 81.04/mo.
" + 1 dependent	$139.92/mo.	$152.37/mo.	$161.62/mo.
" + 2 or more dependents	$203.92/mo.	$228.87/mo.	$244.76/mo.

---

1. What is the most a family of four can save per month under the new plans?
2. What is the range of savings for a family of two under the new plans?
   (from $ _____ to $ _____ per month in savings compared to the old plan)

4 Put It in Writing

Step 1. In small groups, discuss the following three questions.

1. Have you ever had a choice of health-care plans? How do you feel about having such choices?

2. What do you like or dislike about each of the three options described?

3. What additional questions do you have about these health-care plans?

Step 2. Now—as a group or individually—write about choosing a health care plan. Use your discussion of the above questions as "starters." Make lists on a separate sheet of paper for each "starter." Exchange with others when you are finished writing.

Example: Choosing health care in America is _____ for these reasons: _____

Of the three plans here, I like the _____ plan because it has these features: _____

5 Listen and Speak

Step 1. Listen to the conversation.

> A: I'm not sure what I'm going to choose.
>   We have a choice of the PPO, which is the traditional
>   plan, or the HMO, which is cheaper, but it doesn't let you choose
>   your own doctor.
> B: Right. I like the PPO because I'll be able to keep my doctor, who
>   is someone I've been with for years. He's one of the best.
>   But the out-of-pocket costs are hard to predict.
> C: And that high deductible—who needs it? I'll take an HMO. It's simpler.
> A: Maybe you can tell me—how will you find a good doctor from all the
>   choices on these lists?
> C: There's one place close to home. I figure that will be OK.
> D: Can anyone find a pediatrician at one of the medical places on this list?
> C: I think I saw one listed at Brookside.
> B: But is that person any good? You can't tell from a list.
> A: I see they have my pediatrician, who has an office near here.
> D: It *does* say here that you can change doctors. Where's that form?

Step 2. Practice the conversation in a group of four.

Step 3. Continue the conversation until each person helps another answer a different question.

6 Read and Write

Step 1. Read the information about the family below.

Family Information:

Parents: Martha & Ronald Larkins
Children: Tanya & Matthew Larkins

Physicians at Center Number 348

Internal Medicine: Dr. Jaime Rodriguez, M.D.
                    Dr. Fayeda Said, M.D.
                    Dr. Gerard Ponticello, M.D.
Family Practice: Dr. Arleen Kwasnik, M.D.
                    Dr. Frank McDonald, M.D.

Step 2. For this family of four, make up birth dates.

Step 3. Enter their information onto the form below. Then read the list of doctors at Center No. 348. Select one of the doctors, and write his/her name on the form.

MEDICAL INFORMATION

Name _____ M/F _____ Age _____

Height _____ Weight _____ Marital Status _____

Spouse's Name (if applicable) _____

Children

Name	Age	Date of Birth	M/F
1.			
2.			
3.			
4.			
5.			

Physician _____

Step 4. With a partner, compare your work.

Form and Function

1 How much is deducted from our paycheck?

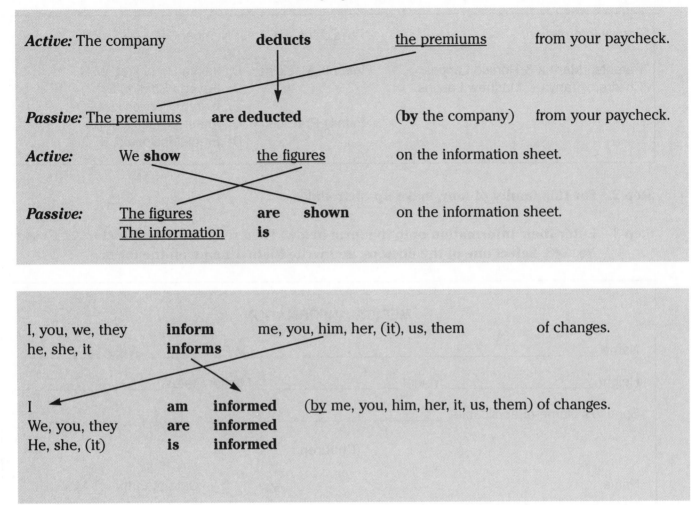

Examples

The insurance **is paid** up through the end of the year. The premiums **are paid** monthly.
All employees at Smithson, Inc., **are covered** by health insurance. I**'m covered**, but Anna **isn't covered**. **Are** you **covered** by the company plan?

Practice 1

A. Listen and circle the words you hear.

1.	covered	(is covered)	**4.**	has done	is done
2.	helped	is helped	**5.**	has shown	is shown
3.	handled	is handled	**6.**	has deducted	is deducted

B. Rewrite the sentences below. Change them from active voice to passive voice. Include a phrase with *by* in each sentence.

1. Algren Insurance provides the traditional health plan for our company.

   The traditional health plan for our company is provided by Algren Insurance.

2. The Personnel Office handles all of the paperwork.

   _____

3. Wendy and I enter all of the information into the computer.

   _____

4. Paperwork takes up a great deal of our time on this job.

   _____

C. Do you have health insurance? If you do, tell a partner about some of the things that are covered under your plan. If you don't have health insurance, talk about the things that are usually covered or that you need.

Examples: Visits to the doctor are covered by my plan.
Hospitalization is covered by most plans, but not at 100 percent of the cost.

2   We have a choice between the PPO, which is the traditional plan, or the HMO, which is cheaper.

Which = things   *Who* = people

We have <u>the PPO</u>,   **which is** the traditional plan,   and <u>the HMO</u>,   **which is** cheaper.
(There is only one.)   (It is the traditional plan.)   (There is only one.)   (It is cheaper.)

There are <u>three PPOs</u>, **which are** the traditional plans, and <u>two HMOs</u>, **which are** cheaper.
(All of the PPOs are the traditional plans.)   (Both of the HMOs are cheaper.)

I hope I can keep <u>my doctor</u>, **who is** one of the best in this area.

Examples

To register for the HMO, you go to <u>the Personnel Office</u>, **which is** the office down the hall on the right. <u>Judy</u>, **who is** the Personnel Manager, can give you the forms.
I decided to take <u>the PPO</u>, **which is** the plan that lets me keep my doctor.
Renata decided not to take the company health plan because she prefers her husband's <u>health plan</u>, **which is** cheaper and **provides** better coverage.

Practice 2

A. Listen twice. The first time, circle the words you hear from the choices on the left. The second time, circle the antecedents.

1. (which is)   which are   **antecedent:** (health plan)   Personnel Office

2. which does   which do   **antecedent:** company   manager

3. which handles   who handles   **antecedent:** president   insurance premiums

4. which covers   who covers   **antecedent:** plan   representative

B. Complete the sentences below with *who* or *which*.

1. The president is Bob Smith, _____*who*_____ has been with the company since 1963.

2. The insurance plan is called HealthPlus, _____ is one of the best available.

3. The person you need to call is Greta Myslitel, _____ is at extension 786.

4. First you fill out the medical history form, _____ you then have to give to the secretary in the Personnel Office.

5. I usually go to the Midtown Health Clinic, _____ is on the corner of Fifth and Madison.

6. Last night we heard a talk by Edwina Hallek, _____ is a local job counselor.

C. Work with a partner. Tell your partner about a company, a person, or a place you know about. Tell who or what the person, company, or place is and give a brief explanation with *who* or *which*.

Examples: My former supervisor was Mary Collins, who was an excellent boss.
Several years ago, I worked at the New York Phone Company, which had a really good health plan.
I used to live in Texas, which is very hot in the summer.

1 Pair Work

Step 1. With a partner, listen to the discussion of the differences between the PPO and the HMO. Make notes in the chart below.

	PPO	HMO
Premiums (for individuals and families)		
Deductible		
Percentage of payment for doctor visits		
Percentage of hospitalization covered		
Dental coverage available?		
Number of doctors, hospitals available under the plan		

Step 2. With your partner, discuss the pros and cons of each plan. List them below.

Plan	Pros	Cons
HMO		
PPO		

Step 3. Think of the kind of coverage you need for your family. With your partner, discuss which plan would be better for you. Discuss the reasons and list them on a separate sheet of paper. Save your work.

2 Group/Class Work

Step 1. Work in a group. Choose a team leader, a team recorder, and a team reporter. Compare your notes on the differences between the HMO and the PPO. Do you have the same information or different information? Try to work out any differences you have.

Step 2. Discuss which plan would be better for each of the members of your group. Discuss your reasons for choosing the plan for each person. Make a chart like the one below:

Person	Plan	Reasons
1.		
2.		
3.		
4.		

Step 3. Your team reporter will tell the class your reasons. Listen to the ideas of the other groups and add your own opinions.

3 Culture Work

With the class, discuss the following questions:

1. Who is responsible for a person's health, the individual, the company, the family, society, or some other group?
2. What is the relationship between the health of the individual and the health of the group? between the health of the individual and the health of society?
3. What kind of responsibility can people take for their own health?
4. What kind of relationship should a person have with his or her doctor?
5. What kind of responsibility should a doctor have toward an individual?
6. What kinds of things can a patient discuss with his or her doctor?
7. What kinds of coverage should a health-care plan provide?

Picture Dictionary

Jobs

doctors (physicians)

firefighters

librarian

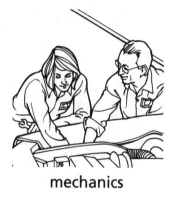

mechanics

office workers

technician

Protective Gear

gloves

goggles

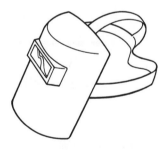

a welding helmet

circular saw

computer
(X-239065564)

drier
(2278676934SJ)

fax machine
(HR-85467-982)

floor buffer
(23044988-LX)

grill
(DGL89345)

oven
(57-3447-8)

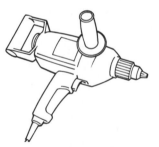

power drill
(89339210064)

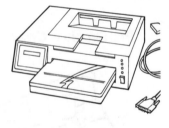

printer
(SXL-98355)

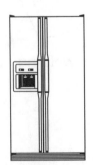

refrigerator
(A-655703-FR)

vacuum cleaner
(860-27)

washing machine
(833307458-J)